GARDENS OF EDEN

GARDENS OF EDEN

British Socialists in the Open Air
1890-1939

Tony Judge

ALPHA HOUSE

ALPHA HOUSE BOOKS

London, England

alphahouse7@gmail.com

copyright@2014 Tony Judge

Revised Edition 2017

All Rights Reserved

ISBN: 9781497489813

Contents

1 FRATERNITY IN THE OPEN AIR

As British socialism struggled to emerge in the late nineteenth century, the form it would eventually take was far from clear. Apart from the advocates of ideological socialism there was an older idealistic form espoused by William Morris and Robert Blatchford among many others, the roots of which stretched back to pre-industrial times. Under the impact of industrialization, it re-emerged in a vision of 'Merrie England' to inspire new ways of living along socialist lines in which industrial production and urban life were anathema. Instead, it was thought self-sufficiency and co-operative communalism, ideally in a rural setting, were the best means to avoid the competitiveness and human alienation of modern capitalism.

Part of this strand of socialism invested the rural and pastoral with a nostalgia for a time of supposed lost innocence, a rural idyll before industrialization and urban growth corrupted it. In this, as in so much else, the main inspiration came from William Morris. In his *News from Nowhere* (1894) Morris outlined a utopian vision of the future firmly set in a rural paradise, unpolluted by the corrupting influences of industrial capitalism. The narrator, William Guest, falls asleep after returning from a meeting of the Socialist League, and awakes to find himself in a new society where equality and cooperation prevail. There are no big cities, and everybody lives in the countryside where there is no private property. Neither are there any factories, but only small workshops and smallholdings where people work just to satisfy their needs. There is no monetary system or governing authority, and social class distinctions have disappeared. It is an agrarian society in which people live at one with nature, satisfying their needs and receiving spiritual and physical refreshment from it.1

John Ruskin was another opponent of industrialism who influenced this kind of socialist nostalgia for the rural open air life. His conviction was that the spiritual and aesthetic sensibilities of working people were being blunted under the impact of industrialism, and needed releasing. They had become alienated in the squalid living and working conditions of the cities where they had ended up in a long exile from village and farm. A keen campaigner for the preservation of the countryside and country life, Ruskin also influenced the popularity of rural tourism with his ideas about scenic 'wilderness'. Although not highly political himself, Ruskin's ideas were mediated for socialist thought through the writings of Morris, and Edward Carpenter.2

The social reformer Octavia Hill was a friend of Ruskin and influenced by his ideas, especially the importance of a green environment for the urban working poor. A staunch opponent of spoliation in the countryside, she campaigned vigorously to preserve the Lake District. Although not a socialist, Hill was influenced by Henry Mayhew's survey of the living conditions of the London poor and by the Christian Socialism of F.D. Maurice, working for a time at his London Workingmen's College. Hill's main work was in the provision of social housing for the poorest of urban workers, and Ruskin provided the initial investment for her first social housing project in Marylebone. But she was also concerned about the spiritual welfare of her tenants, and their need to have access to green open spaces. Sharing with her socialist contemporaries belief in the benign effect of 'the life enhancing virtues of pure earth, clean air and blue sky', she campaigned for the preservation of Hampstead Heath and Parliament Hill Fields in North London, saving them from development. The needs of the poor for green open spaces seemed obvious to her:

> And what is it precisely that should be given? I think we want four things. Places to sit in, places to play in, places to stroll in, and places to spend a day in. The preservation of Wimbledon (Common) and Epping (Forest) shows that the need is increasingly recognized. But a visit to Wimbledon, Epping or Windsor, ‚means for the workman not only the cost of the journey but the loss of a whole days wages: we want, besides, places where the long summer evenings or Saturday afternoons may be enjoyed without effort or expense.3

In 1876 the Kyrle Society was founded by Hill's sister Miranda as a 'Society for the Diffusion of Beauty', and Octavia became its treasurer. The aim was to bring art, books, music, and open spaces into the lives of the urban masses with the slogan 'Beauty, Home to the Poor'. This became the blueprint for the future National Trust in ways that Octavia might not have entirely approved.

The vision of a 'Merrie England' that was found in the work of William Morris and John Ruskin was given further resonance by Robert Blatchford in his widely read book of the same name. Blatchford was a socialist and polemical journalist, well-practiced in seeming to speak directly to his readers. He also proposed an ideal society in the countryside, uncorrupted by the effects of industrial capitalism. The people would work contentedly in small workshops and on smallholdings, self-sufficient to meet the needs of the village communities, free from the need to maximize production for capitalist profits. This would allow them plenty of leisure to enrich their lives with cultural pursuits and healthy outdoor activities such as walking, rowing, swimming and football.[4]

Blatchford's vision was steeped in a nostalgia for a past in that it was assumed working people enjoyed a more natural relationship with each other, and with their surroundings. He wanted people to recapture the supposed lost innocence of the pre-industrial world, and create socialist communities from the grass-roots up rather than imposed from above by state or central government. Blatchford was always suspicious of bureaucratic and centralized political organization and, although involved in the formation of the Independent Labour Party, had little time for the trade unions or the new Labour Party when it was formed. He thought the people should have better things to do with their spare time than political campaigning, and even that should be undertaken with a sense of fun and never out of duty.

This was the basis of the Clarion movement which he and his newspaper inspired, 'a sociable socialism' more like a 'family gathering, a brotherly – and sisterly, if you like – jollification, not a political conference.'[5] After the working day or week was over the pursuit of healthy past times in the open air was recommended, and these were contrasted to unhealthy and lowering activities found in the industrial cities such as drinking, gambling, and pub games in smoky crowded interiors. Blatchford loved the countryside, escaped to it whenever he could, and filled his columns in the *Clarion* with articles extolling rural life and short-stories set in rural locations. These often made the contrast, actual or implied, between the living and working conditions of the northern industrial towns where most of the readers lived, and the benefits of rural life. The movement that he inspired was dedicated to cycling, handicrafts, camping, and open air activities of all kinds as well as socialist campaigning.

An example of this community activism were the Clarion Vans which visited the poorer parts of the country dispensing hot soup together with a socialist message. Several cities had a Clarion Van, painted with the Clarion logo and political messages. In Liverpool, with Julia Dawson as the organizing force, it was particularly active in the city and in touring all over the North West. Several annual tours were undertaken, in 1896 starting at Chester it proceeded through Shropshire, Staffordshire, Derbyshire, Lancashire and Yorkshire before ending up in Durham. The send-off in Chester included members of the Clarion Cycling Club and a brass-band playing the Marseillaise. It was a wet summer but the rain did not dampen the lively spirits, and there were many stops and speeches.[5]

The Clarion Van movement spread and their tours went all over the country, some deep into the countryside. The tour of the West country in 1907 started at Barnstable on 29 February before the van made its way through the villages and market towns of Devon. In almost all the villages there were large crowds eager to hear about the new politics of socialism. The local farmers and landowners, all Tories, tried to stop their workers attending and heckled the speakers loudly singing 'God Save the King'. By April the van had reached Exeter via Newton Abbot and again huge crowds gathered hear the Clarion speakers.[6]

The theme of access to the land for the working class had already become an important one in socialist propaganda. The tradition of agrarian socialism went back to the Digger movement in the seventeenth century, and the name indicated that its members wished to farm the common land. The original name of the Levellers derived from their belief in economic and social equality, based on extracts from the New Testament. They wanted an agrarian way of life on small self-sufficient communities, such as those they set up at Wellingborough, Iver, and at Little Heath near Chobham in Surrey. The leader, Gerrard Winstanley and his original followers believed that "true freedom lies where a man receives his nourishment and preservation, and that is in the use of the earth." [7]

The narrative that the land had once been the peoples by birthright, and had then been 'stolen' from them was familiar from *Merrie England,* expounded by Keir Hardie, and elaborated in books such as J.L. Hammond's *The Village Labourer.* There were still many signs of the old 'Merrie England' existing in the countryside before 1914, and that could encourage thoughts of returning to the land. Sleepy villages with thatched cottages, un-spoilt village greens, little churches and farmer's markets still abounded. Vast areas of the countryside were still 'unspoilt' and in a 'natural' state with many independent small farmers, and the power of the landowning gentry still largely intact.

By the 1920's commercial and industrial developments were encroaching, and by the 1930's the countryside was seriously under threat. This created an imperative for socialist organizations to re-energize their campaign for access to the land, and the protection of it for leisure purposes. The propaganda of the Left at this time emphasized the malign influence of capitalism, turning a nation of free people into property-less urban wage slaves. The landlessness and insecurity of the urban working class provided a powerful and emotional propaganda weapon. The 'theft' of the land from the 'common people' still remained the theme, with the need to redress ancient wrongs by redistribution and re-settlement, calling for land nationalization, creation of national parks, new towns and planning.8

Many younger socialists in particular preferred to combine their political activities with enjoying the pleasures of the countryside, and this involved group activities like cycling, rock climbing, rambling, camping and attending summer schools. The idealization of the countryside encouraged this by projecting it as a place to refresh the spirit, a theme of Morris and Blatchford, as well as a kind of Arcadian playground. This view was endorsed by the Clarion movement, and Labour Party leaders like Keir Hardie and Ramsay MacDonald. The latter believed that young men and women should be initiated into 'the love of the hills and the physical endurance which is the homage exacted by the hills, is as necessary as to initiate them into Marxian economics'9

The urban scene was represented as unhealthy and demeaning, with people unable to realize their full potential as human beings, while the material benefits of urban life – employment, higher wages and living standards – were played down. MacDonald regarded being in the great outdoors as an essential part of political education, and believed in a strong link between being politically progressive and being inspired by nature and landscape. The William Morris dream in the 1880s of every working man being only a few minutes walk from the countryside, remained a consistent theme on the Left. It was still being echoed in 1933 by Hugh Dalton when he asserted that a sign of an uncivilized community was when every inhabitant could not reach open country, or find a public space, after a moderate walk or drive.10

The attraction of socialism to many lay in this antagonism to urban life, and to those aspects of industrial capitalism it personified. Robert Blatchford was eloquent in his frequent anti-urban diatribes in the pages of the *Clarion* against the northern factory and mill towns where his eponymous everyman, John Smith, lived and to whom *Merrie England* was addressed. He wrote that the "ugliness of Widnes and Sheffield and the beauty of Monsal Dale are not matters of sentiment – they are matters of fact."11 This ugliness and squalor had a debilitating effect on the aesthetic sensibilities of a large number of the inhabitants, he claimed, and it was this as much as their economic exploitation as wage labourers and factory fodder, that should incense socialists.

Many on the Left came to believe that the growth of urbanization, factory production and materialism had become irreversible, and for some the only hope was for groups to create their own small socialist utopias. In the 1880s and 1890s these proliferated across the country aiming to be harmonious, communal and self-sufficient. They involved market-gardening, farming, arts and crafts, and small-scale manufacturing, but all were an attempt to some extent to cut themselves off from the capitalist system, and live lives according to higher values. This type of socialist idealism had some sympathizers in the Independent Labour Party, the Socialist League and the Socialist Democratic Federation, but was regarded unsympathetically by the Fabians. It was in conflict with their rational scientific approach to socialism, gradualist reforms based on research, the accumulation of evidence and campaigning pressure.

In contrast to the overcrowding and pollution of the towns, the green and pleasant aura of the countryside symbolized the merits of better life for all in the open air. The Left appropriated the merits of country life as symbols of socialist virtue, and thereby as a means of inspiring people's commitment to socialist goals. Political education should take the form of cycling excursions, rambles, hikes, camps and summer schools, or setting up cooperative rural communities, and extended to the idea of planned garden cities. The aim was the same: utilizing rural amenities to show what socialism and community could mean, and to provide a template for creating a better world in the future.

It has been argued that in the late nineteenth century a 'religion of socialism' emerged, when the movement was characterized by 'the sheer pleasure of fraternity' and incorporated activities that had previously been alien from to it. This led to a unifying of socialism with other aspects of life, including leisure activities.12 By the 1890's the labour movement was aware of the importance of leisure, and it was assumed that the most edifying form it could take was in the open-air. The 'right to leisure' came to be seen as standing side by side with 'the right to work' and with access to the countryside just as necessary in creating a proper socialist society.

The countryside was also seen as being more conducive to clear-thinking, where the problems of the world were more likely to be resolved. The design of the new socialist future would benefit from being planned well away from all the diversions of the urban world. In providing a suitably sylvan setting to facilitate this, the early Labour Party benefited from the patronage of a few wealthy benefactors and sympathizers with large country houses to place at the disposal of the party. But these grand country houses, with their parks and gardens, were symbols of social class privilege and power through the ownership of land. They may have been planned by fashionable garden designers, but were made by the labour of masses of workers from the estates and villages in the area. To many early socialists they also symbolized what had been lost to the people, the theft of the land turned into private privilege and ownership. The irony of early Labour leaders being guests in a few of these houses might not have been lost on them, discussing socialism while peacocks flitted by on the terraces, and servants seeing to their needs. This taste of a privileged country lifestyle may even have given a few the taste for an aristocratic lifestyle, but confirmed for others their socialist convictions and the need for change.

The gardens of these houses represented not only what had been lost through economic and social change, but were also symbolic of the future that socialism could offer. The symbol of the Garden of Eden was used in this way by William Morris in 'A Dream of John Bull,' which first appeared in the *Communard* in 1886-1887, based on the peasants revolt of 1381. The 1888 edition was illustrated by Edward Burne Jones, including 'Where Adam and Eve spun, who was the gentleman?' The picture imagines a time, present and in the future, where there is no class-system, and the Garden of Eden a place where labour is not alienated but at peace with the environment. In developing his vision in *News From Nowhere*, Morris portrayed work as something that should be a pleasurable experience and a communal effort towards "the utmost refinement of workmanship" enabling freedom of fancy and imagination. He chooses the garden as the place where this freedom is extended, a place of cultivated beauty enjoyed by the gardener and visitor alike.13

When Adam delved and Eve span who was then the gentleman

1 Edward Burne-Jones, 'When Adam delved and Eve span who was the gentleman. Illustration for William Morris' 'A Dream of John Bull' 1888

Another socialist artist and illustrator who used flowers, plants and fruit in this way was Walter Crane, whose political cartoons and illustrations provided much of the visual iconography of early socialism. Like other early socialists he wanted to see a disfigured society transformed into beauty, and *A Floral Fantasy in an English Garden* of 1899 includes floral verses celebrating the arrival of Spring. The book was inspired by Crane's visits to the gardens at Easton Lodge in Essex, owned by 'Daisy Greville, the Countess of Warwick. She had been converted to socialism by Robert Blatchford, after he had criticized her opulent lifestyle as a "callousness that mocks and laughs at misery."14Daisy planted her garden in the 1880's, and Crane made several visits in the 1890's as he became friendly with her as a fellow socialist. She had inherited the estate from her grandfather, and set about creating a deer park and a series of themed gardens, including the 'Daisy Garden, the 'Friendship Garden' and the 'Shakespeare Garden.

In *Floral Fantasy* Crane did not specifically illustrate the garden at Easton Lodge, but used his own symbolism it inspired. The political system is shown in the first image of the garden with a red-headed fairy wearing a cap of liberty, opening the garden gate for an artisan to enter. Then, strolling around the garden he sees flowers in human form, and the tour ends with the setting of the sun. This image had been used by Crane earlier in 1897 with an angel handing the key of a garden to a labourer, symbolizing the landless and poor enjoying the rights of access to the beauties of nature when the socialist society arrives.15Crane used the symbolism of the garden to represent the bounties of nature that had been denied to the people, and would be restored to them with the coming of socialism. In his illustration for the cover of the prospectus of Louise Michel's International School, started during her exile in London between 1890-95, there is a beautiful maiden distributing fruit freely from a tree to a child, with the framing messages of socialism around the picture.

The idyllic garden scene could not hide the fact that the workers who labored in gardens, orchards and farms were overworked and underpaid. Crane was well aware of this, and saw the evidence when visiting Easton Lodge. In 1900 Daisy commissioned the fashionable designer Harold Peto to remodel the gardens, and offered the hard laboring work to the Salvation Army, no doubt with good intentions.

2 Walter Citrine's illustration for the prospectus of Louise Michel's International School

Sixty-seven local homeless and unemployed men were deployed to make the formal lawns, the yew walk, wooden pagodas, and the round pond according to Peto's designs. To Crane, it seemed that while the new garden provided work for the unemployed, it could also be a place of exploitation, decadence and conspicuous consumption, as well as beauty and freedom for a few. This situation would remain until the rights of private property ownership and the privileges it entailed were reformed. In his view these garden paradises should not be escapes from the real world, but help lead to radical political reform.16

In the late nineteenth century, with the development of local government in cities like Glasgow, Birmingham and London, the Victorian public park was developed further, and gave urban workers the chance to enjoy nature and be in the open air. The growth of allotment provision in towns and cities also afforded the opportunity for them to cultivate crops and, temporarily at least, be in touch with the soil. This was the experiencing of nature at an urban or suburban remove, but provided refreshment for the spirit and opportunity for healthy pastimes. Those socialists who wanted to put their principles into practice joined communal land settlements in the countryside, with several established in the 1890s of various sizes and types, some floundering while others flourished.

This seemingly more innocent world might have ended with the advent of war in 1918, and the mounting casualties on the Western Front. But socialist idealism lived on, and during the Great War found expression for some on the Left in pacifism and conscientious objection. They faced the threat of imprisonment, or at least abuse, and some needed a safe haven where they could lie low and hope to avoid the attention of the authorities for a time. These places were mainly in the countryside, often in remote areas such as North Wales, where the young socialist Cyril Joad found sanctuary as a conscious objector in the summer of 1916. He was on indefinite leave from his civil service post without pay while the authorities considered his case, and he went to stay at Bryn Corach near Conway.

This was the headquarters of the Holiday Fellowship founded by T.A. Leonard, a fellow pacifist and Christian Socialist, to provide low cost holidays in 'wild' places amid great scenic beauty for the urban working class. The holiday centres also occasionally provided refuge for young conscientious objectors in flight from the authorities, and Joad was given temporary employment as a guide for groups of young 'townees' climbing Mount Snowden. It meant he was away when officials called looking for him, and so could not issue him with a summons.

He enjoyed taking these groups of mainly young people, usually working or lower middle class from northern towns, into the spectacular scenery of Snowdonia. He was amazed at how they were transformed by their experience of the mountains, and became more co-operative and united in the beautiful but testing surroundings. They usually had no previous experience of mountain-climbing but learnt quickly how to survive and seemed to find new energy in pitching tents, cooking, and doing the washing-up. It confirmed for Joad the emancipating influence of exposure to the countryside, and the transformative effects it could have on urban people.[17]

Socialist idealism of this kind was typical in the making of a close identity between the countryside and the beneficial effects on people, helping them reach a truer level of humanity. It was in the countryside, and in 'wild' and 'un-spoilt' landscapes in particular, that more honest relationships could be nurtured, and social class distinctions dissolve amid the need for cooperation and communal effort. The suffering and slaughter war might have shaken this kind of idealism, but it actually made Joad and his generation on the Left all the more determined to pursue their aims, not least in trying to ensure that such a catastrophe never occurred again by demonstrating the futility and waste of competitive individualism.

There were also socialists, or potential socialist voters, who lived and worked in the countryside and could hardly share in any idealized view of it. Those working on the land suffered during the great agricultural depressions of the 1880s, and in the slumps between the wars. They faced low wages, long hours and tied cottage accommodation from which they could be removed any time by the farmer or landowners agent. In 1920 the abolition of minimum price guarantees, soon after being introduced, plunged some farmers into crisis and much of rural society with them. The market was flooded with cheap foreign food, and many smaller farmers were ruined, with abandoned farms and even whole villages in parts of Norfolk, Suffolk and Essex.

Most of this decline was in cereal farming, but one way to survive was to band together in a farming cooperative and there were some remarkable cooperative successes in the 1930s, notably the Preston and District Trading Society. This group of local poultry farmers was so successful that by 1931 it was producing one-third of all eggs for the British market. The Co-operative Wholesale Society farms used vertical integration and economies of scale to prosper and there was the success of the John Lewis Partnership-owned Lethbridge cooperative farm in Hampshire as well as some smaller buying cooperatives or partial cooperative goups.18

There were also socialist experiments in land settlement which were also run on co-operative and communal principles, usually on a self-sufficiency basis, although there were exceptions run on more commercial lines supplying the wholesale or retail markets. The hope was these would provide some relief from agricultural and urban unemployment, that by the 1930s had become a major economic and social problem. There was a decline of 10% in farming jobs between 1921 and 1931, and a further 15% decline between 1930 and 1938 even though the rural population was increasing. This decline led the Labour Party and the farm workers unions to try to radicalize the workers, and encourage them to question the status quo and social hierarchy of the countryside. To an extent the policy succeeded, and the National Union of Agricultural Workers hoped to exploit the situation by using grievances over low ages, insecurity of housing and employment. These problems were not new, nor was the hostility of farmers to trade union membership and activity, or the tied-cottage system. The latter was a constant irritant, as were the Wages Boards, and the union spent a great deal of time and resources defending its members interests at tribunal hearings.[19]

The Labour Party also set out to court the rural vote between the wars with promises to make farming and the countryside prosperous, improve the lives of farm workers, and revive village life. At the same time socialists, not all of them in the Labour Party, continued to see the countryside as representing a 'Merrie England', an idealized playground for the pleasure and edification of the urban workers. This did not always sit easily with the poverty of those who actually worked and lived in the countryside. By the 1920s the Labour Party was proposing schemes for improving rural infrastructure, communications, housing and transport, and even land nationalization. But the socialist nostalgia for a more traditional way of life was still alive even in the 1930s when Stafford Cripps, speaking at a trade union rally, could still lament the passing of 'the old culture of the countryside, with its music and dancing, with its feats, fairs and shows.[20]

The potential conflict between policies intended to improve the countryside and lives of country dwellers, and those for increasing access and preserving the landscape, were never entirely resolved. They tended to get mixed up, and as late as 1936 the Labour Party was publishing a 'Plan to Make the Countryside a Glorious Picture' with an image of teams of horses at work ploughing the fields. At the same time the document contained proposals or raising farm workers wages and other improvements, and contained images that showed the countryside still seen in idealistic and aesthetic terms as a place in which it was a joy to live.[21]

But there was a great deal of regeneration of the social and educational side of rural life going on between the wars. Some were private initiatives such as Conrad Noel and the Thaxted Community experiment, which saw a remarkable resurgence of village life and community spirit in one Essex village, and also in the work of the Workers Education Association. The WEA was very active in the countryside after 1924 when it became a 'responsible body' for grant aid purposes under the 1918 Education Act. It set about providing one and three year courses for working-class people at the university level. There was a close relationship with some university extension departments, as in the Devon Extension Scheme of 1927 in association with the University College of the South West, described as a 'voyage of discovery into the realms of the spirit; a quest for the "eternal verities" of life.'16 Meeting in village halls and school rooms all over the country WEA tutors did bring new vistas of knowledge into people's lives which, according to the aims of the WEA, was the human right of all the working class.

From the 1890s to the 1930s there was a sustained growing interest in hygiene and physical fitness, running parallel to the open-air movement. There were a range of groups who were dedicated to health and physical culture activities, usually in the open-air, whose members were by no means all on the left. The socialists generally believed that the pursuit of healthy activities in the countryside would encourage fraternity, cooperation, and unity, paving the way to a fairer and more equal society. However, some members of the health and fitness movement had other priorities, concerned with creating a healthier and physically-fit population more able to combat external and internal threats. Unlike the socialists, they were given some official encouragement connected to the needs of the modern state for a healthy, fit and disciplined citizenry. This partly underlay the welfare reforms of the pre-war 1914 Liberal government and the support of the National government in the 1930s.

But there were other less benign motives in the health and fitness movement that included eugenicists who feared racial degeneration, and sympathizers for the fascist regimes in Europe with their desire for a disciplined and fit population. A trend in the 1930s was the wish In some quarters to create citizenship categories based on health and physical well-being. Less threatening was the growth in the popularity of vegetarianism, sunbathing, hiking, keep-fit classes and sport of all kinds. These were also popular among socialists, as well as promoted by the governments 'National Fitness Campaign' from 1935.The monarch, George V, was involved in sponsoring several groups promoting the outdoor recreation including swimming, camping, and hiking, all part of the flowering outdoor leisure culture of the 1930's.[22]

The left shared in this new culture but tended to plough its own furrow, not least because it sought to change society rather than just reinforce the status-quo. Many socialists felt the need to do this by community-based activism, demonstrating what could be achieved by cooperation. The Clarion Clubs enjoyed a revival partly because of it, as did other socialist and communist groups of all kinds dedicated to sport and other activities in the open-air. They included the youth sections of the Labour and Communist parties, as well as non-aligned socialist groups and sympathizers. They were involved in rambling, canoeing, football, athletics and many other sports. Their activities also included education, self-improvement and non-sporting leisure and vacation activities in the open-air. There was a renewed urgency and energy in some of this activity, perhaps arising from a feeling that with little prospect of a socialist government and another war increasingly likely, it was up to the younger generation of socialists to enjoy the countryside and open air with all it had to offer in constructive leisure activity.

2 CLARION CLUBS

The first edition of Robert Blatchford's weekly socialist newspaper, the *Clarion,* was published on 12 December 1891. It was intended by its founders to promote a new form of journalism, free from editorial restrictions and in a close contact with its readers. The nearest it came to an editorial policy was contained in its first leader in which Blatchford asserted that the policy of the paper was "not of party, sect or creed; but of justice, of reason and mercy."[1] From the outset it adopted a breezy humorous style with an underlying seriousness. Partly due to its unconventional approach, and its independence from political parties, it became an effective propaganda force for socialism. It was able to benefit from the growth of the trade union movement and wider literacy, reaching a circulation of 74,000 mainly working class readers in the northern cities and towns.[2]

The *Clarion* was a campaigning newspaper, and tried to maintain a higher moral tone than its more down-market rivals, even though it had to have its popular features. These included sports reports, especially association football teams based in the northern towns like Preston North End, Blackburn Rovers and Bolton Wanderers. Their matches were reported weekly for local readers, as well as gossip about clubs and their players. In the summer there was reporting of Lancashire county cricket from Old Trafford and on Yorkshire's matches. Test matches were reported in depth together with the local cricket league matches on both sides of the Pennines.

The combination of serious politics, sport, social gossip, light verse, cartoons, drama, and music reviews, as well as stories proved a highly successful mix for a time. Its large circulation boosted the sales of Blatchford's socialist tract *Merrie England,* which sold cheaply priced copies in huge numbers. This attacked the iniquities of factory labour and its exploitation, but also idealized self-sufficiency in a rural setting. In anideal society people were envisaged as living in small village communities, working on smallholdings, or in small craft-based workshops. They would feel part of the land and at one with the products they produced. There would be plenty of leisure without capitalist employers imposing long hours of work, plenty of time for the enjoyment of healthy country pursuits in the open air.3

The *Clarion* was much more than a newspaper for it gave rise to a remarkable mass movement. Blatchford encouraged the formation of a range of organizations whose members wanted to combine pursuing an interest having a good time, and campaigning for socialism. The mainly young activists joined groups of Clarion Cyclists, Scouts, Field Clubs, Rambling, Swimming, Handicrafts, Choirs and Cinderella Clubs, among others, most of which involved getting young people out of the towns.

The most popular of all were the Clarion Cycling Clubs, the first of which was formed in February 1894 in Birmingham. Later that year clubs were formed in Liverpool, Stoke and Barnsley, and by 1895 there were thirty clubs, while by 1897 the number had risen to seventy. They were so popular because cycling enabled people of modest means to access and explore the countryside. The price of a second-hand bicycle was within the reach of the employed working class, and some were able to save up for a new one, handing down the old one to a younger member. Freedom and mobility was the aim, and within a group of like-minded people.

A National Clarion Cycling Club (NCCC) was formed with a masthead designed by Walter Crane, who was already well-known for his illustrations in the paper. The goals of the NCCC were to organize cyclists 'for Mutual Aid, Good Fellowship, and the Propagation of the Principles of Socialism, along with the social pleasures of Cycling'. The organization helped to co-ordinate the activities of local Clarion clubs, encourage the formation of new branches, provide insurance against injury and repairs, and promote the whole culture of cycling lore. There was a strong social element to the clubs, and many life-long friendships were made, including marriages. The Liverpool branch was particularly active, and its secretary was soon writing in the *Clarion* seeking new members:

Today we met at Newsham Park at 10am, proceeded to Cronton through Knotty Ash, Broad Green, Huyton, Roby and Tarbuck. We distributed literature and had a most enjoyable picnic. Returned to Liverpool about 2.00 am I hope all Clarionettes cyclists will join us, and spread the good news among the heathen. As for those who haven't a 'bike' let them sell their shirts and buy one. PS Next Sunday's run to Chester meet at Birkenhead boat pier at 2.00 pm.4

In 1894 Blatchford suggested in his 'Nunquam' column that a cycling corps of Clarion scouts might be formed to carry the socialist message far and wide on their travels. That summer a meeting of the Birmingham and Potteries Clarion Club decided to act on this suggestion. The main aim of the Clarion Scouts was to use the cycling trips to spread the socialist message by distributing leaflets and other literature, including copies of the *Clarion*, in the villages and towns through which they passed. The same year saw a section of the Clarion Scouts established in Liverpool, and they immediately started distributing socialist propaganda, taking special satisfaction doing so in a village on the estate of the Earl of Derby. They reported their adventures in the columns of the paper:

> Just concluded two splendid runs – from Knowsley where his lordship the Earl of Derby did not invite us to dinner, but his tenants were supplied with Clarions and Clarion leaflets. We also called at the Police Station and left some tracts for the edification of the gentlemen in blue. After assimilating the cowjuice we returned home. In the afternoon several had a spin to Heswell. Here we discovered three Clarionettes and after fraternizing with, also enjoying a good tea and distributing some Clarion leaflets, we made tracks for Birkenhead, arriving at Liverpool at eight o'clock. Next Sunday meet at Newsham Park gates at 10.00am for a run to Cronton.5

So great was the enthusiasm that they started their own journal *The Scout*, subtitled *A Monthly Journal for Socialist Workers*. The first edition in March 1895 contained Blatchford's 'Instructions for Scouts,' giving guidance about door-to-door canvassing, political leafleting, and selling copies of *Merrie England*. They were urged to 'permeate' mines, factories and other work places, convert their workmates to socialism, and do what they could to form branches of the Social Democratic Federation or ILP in their own districts if none already existed. They were also encouraged to write letters to the press, ask questions at political meetings, and help socialist candidates in their campaigns by canvassing or in any other way. Blatchford advised them to always remain calm, polite and good-humored, qualities he valued highly always detesting the rough and tumble of party politics. These instructions were a blueprint on how to make a grass-roots community from the bottom upwards. The project might take decades, but Blatchford believed it was the only way to create a really authentic mass-movement going which could eventually be a permanent affirmation of socialism by the people.6

Cycling came to be regarded as the quintessential socialist outdoors activity by many in the Clarion movement, although at this time it was also enormously popular with the middle classes, most of whom were not socialists but could more easily afford to buy a new bicycle. To the Clarion Scouts their bikes was essential to spread the socialist message, and *The Scout* encouraged its readers to draw up lists of speakers, and then cycle between twenty and fifty miles at weekends to address meetings in places with no socialist organization. Some branches, as in Liverpool, made stickers and labels about four by two inches with gummed reverse sides they could stick on walls, tree-trunks, gateposts, and even an occasional passing cow. They were even supplied with stencil sets to print their own slogans. The Liverpool branch was larger than average and sold 5,000 copies of *Merrie England,* hawking it around the pubs and clubs, including selling it at football matches in the city.7

The practice of sticking labels everywhere did not meet with the approval of the socially conservative Blatchford, as he made clear in his editorial notes:

> I see Candid One in the *Scout* approves of the fashion of sticking labels on things. I must say that I don't like the idea and never did. If I saw any kind of labels – socialist, religious, or what nor – stuck on the rocks and trees, I am sure I would not be pleased. And do you think much good can come of it? If a man sees these labels plastered over the woods and hills, is he not more likely to be angry at the defacement of Nature than be edified by the matter the labels bear?8

As the number of Clarion Cycling Clubs grew, club-houses were established to enable the members to go for cheap weekend excursions out of the town, and further into the countryside. The social element on these trips was always strong, often more so than the political activity. But whatever the motivation, the idea among the mainly young people was always to have a good time. This was in line with Blatchford's belief that political activity was more effective if undertaken with a smile and a joke. The first club-house was a caravan set up in Knutsford in August 1895, which followed a successful three-week camp at Tabley Brook that summer. This consisted of four bell-tents, a square kitchen tent and a large marquee for dining and recreation. All the equipment, some of which was donated by the ILP, was transported to the site by a horse-drawn caravan borrowed from a local farmer and supporter, William Ranstead. This first camp was highly popular with over 2200 cyclists visiting, of whom 460 stayed on for a longer stay.9 The communal living and cooking arrangements gave them the chance to put their co-operative ideals into practice, if only for a short time. It was a simple life, but healthy and free from the materialism and trivia of capitalist society. No alcohol was allowed, and the strongest beverage available was tea, although smoking at the time was perfectly acceptable. The physical effort of cycling to the camp, then sleeping under canvas invariable weather, was part of the experience of being close to nature.

3 Walter Crane's design for the emblem of the National Clarion Cycling Club

Following this success the secretary of the Manchester Clarion Cycling Club, Charlie Reekie, suggested that camps be established in other parts of the country under the slogan 'Comradeship and Fresh Air at a Reasonable Cost.' and wrote a short poem in 1895 for *The Scout* to emphasize the point:

> *Where thrushes sing and busy bee hums*
> *Far from the stinking stifling slums*
> *We'll pitch our tents by a troutlet stream,*
> *Sink all our sorrow, nor think of the morrow*
> *But look on life as a happy dream*

The success of the camp encouraged the Manchester Clarionettes to think about the possibility of finding a permanent club-house in the countryside, perhaps an old farm house that could be purchased cheaply and converted. *The Scout* reported in November 1895 that the Burnley Clarion Club had already established one, and Manchester wanted their own as soon as possible. But by the summer of 1896 they had still not done so, and were again camping at Tabley Brook with fourteen bell-tents and two marquees. Visitors came to stay from as far away as Birmingham and London, one of whom was Keir Hardie who stayed the night and helped make the breakfast in the morning. It rained that year and everything got soaked including the campers, so all thoughts turned to finding a permanent base.10

For some Clarionettes the ideal was to have a club-house modeled on William Morris's *News From Nowhere,* with clean well-appointed rooms, balconies for al fresco meals, fruit orchards and playing fields. Some others had already acted upon this vision such as T.A Leonard whose Holiday Association set up a guest house at Ambleside in 1893. Then in June 1897 the Manchester Clarion Cycling Club finally acquired a bungalow at Bucklow Hill, 'the first experimental co-operative cottage of the Clarion Clubs,' which had a field for camping and playing football. It was taken on a five-year lease from Earl Egetonof Tatton, and was officially opened on 22 June 1897. The aimwas to provide socialists with plenty of healthy open air activities, and alternatives to the celebrations for Victoria's 60th anniversary on the throne.

The opening of the new clubhouse was marked by a ride from Trafford Bar in Manchester to Bucklow Hill, starting at 10am. The opening ceremony was supposed to have been conducted by Robert Blatchford, but he had to cancel and was replaced by J. Pitt Hardacre, the actor-manager of the Comedy Theatre in Manchester, who was an enthusiastic Clarion cyclist. Over 250 stayed for the dinner, and the place overflowed with people onto the balcony and in the grounds. They sat about on deckchairs, and there were tents pitched in the adjoining field to cope with the overflow. There was plenty of room for storing bikes, a large kitchen, dining room, reading room and an office. The dormitories were named after flowers, symbolizing the Arcadian nature of the enterprise, and according to the secretary of the Bolton Clarion Cycling Club the new clubhouse was the centre "of a cycling paradise, away from the smoky towns."12

The club-house proved highly popular, and was used extensively at the weekends and during holidays. The running costs were intended to be met by selling shares at 5/- each in a company organized by Dr. Richard Pankhurst, father of Sylvia and prominent in the Manchester ILP. But it was undersubscribed, and thereafter it became something of a struggle to finance the club-house, and fundraising events had to be organized such as concerts. However, the aristocratic landlord had not realized his new tenants were socialists, and refused to renew the lease in 1902.13

After a delay, a replacement club-house was found in a dilapidated old farmhouse in the countryside between Cheadle and Handforth. This was opened in September 1903, and a much-loved visitor was Edward Fay, the popular 'Bounder' columnist from the *Clarion,* who often accompanied the Clarionettes on their campaigns to spread the socialist message. With much hard-work the place was made comfortable with a sitting-room, dining-room, as well as a library and reading-room. Sleeping accommodation was provided in four dormitories with fifty beds, and tents were available for pitching in the fields. There was a well-cultivated flower garden, a kitchen garden, an orchard and even an open-air theatre where productions ranging from Shakespeare to Shaw were performed. In addition, there were tennis courts, cricket and football matches and an annual s sports day held in July.14

This clubhouse became an important centre for the growth of early socialism in the North-West of England, and popular with Clarion cyclists. They used it as a base for exploring further into the countryside, and people came to stay from all over the industrial towns of the North. For many years it enjoyed a reputation as a haven and a welcoming community, but the mass unemployment of the early 1930s meant this experiment in communal living had to close. There was a further effort to revive the concept in 1936 when another was opened at Valley House, only two miles away, and this remained in existence until 1951. Many people had fond memories of the happy times enjoyed in this cycling fraternity, including the later leader of the women's suffrage movement, Sylvia Pankhurst. Later in life she recalled joining the Clarion Cycling Club in Manchester in 1896 as a 14 year old, every Sunday going on regular rides into the countryside, and getting to know all the writers on the *Clarion* and their pen-names, being taught to ride a bike and enjoying many excursions usually ending with a cream tea. Many friendships were made at the club, and members helped each other to mend punctures, do other repairs and teach the younger ones how to ride a bike or to push them up steep hills when necessary.16

Sylvia also recalled the good humour of the Clarionettes, the songs they sang, and their joyous cries as they careered down country lanes on their bikes. She speculated that this may have had something to do with their optimistic feelings that a brighter future was just around the corner, and the arrival of a socialist society imminent. They were confident this would happen during their lifetime, and encouraged in this feeling of optimism by the *Clarion,* which also emphasized the hard work needed to replace the capitalist system.17

The enthusiasm of these young people, their optimism and social idealism, helped to establish socialism in those parts of the country where the Labour Party would later be strong. But the work of converting the people was never fully completed, as Blatchford saw it, and the creation of a mass grassroots socialist movement remained an unfinished project. But the Clarion members were remarkably politicized at a young age, and this was fostered by the pleasures of being out and about in the fresh country air, made plain in this personal account of involvement:

We were furnished with sandwiches, a primus stove for making tea and stacks of
 Leaflets, pamphlets and the *Clarion.* Leaflets and pamphlets we gave away; the
Clarion we tried to sell. Arriving at some village in Derbyshire or Cheshire we held
an open-air meeting to catch the people as they came out of church or chapel.
We were young and raw and given to buffoonery. There was a tradition that one
Clarion group had posted some posters with the legend 'Read the Clarion' on a
herd of cows in a field. We scrawled slogans in chalk on barns and farmhouse
walls…We sand '*England arise, the long night is over*' outside pubs and on village
greens.
At the clubhouse, after a ride through the lanes of Cheshire or over the
Derbyshire hills, we ate an enormous tea of ham, pickles, jam and
cake…..washing up followed, after which we cleared the tables away for either a
meeting, a play or a concert, finishing the evening by dancing…By ten o'clock
we were shooting down Schools Hill, bunches of wild flowers tied to our handle
bars, apples in our pockets, and the wind lifting our hair." 18

The more prominent Clarionettes went on the become leading socialists activists in their community, such as Robert 'Bob' Mason in Liverpool. He was active in politics in the city for over forty years, and founded and led the annual 'Pezzers Rally', a nocturnal ramble over the fields of the Wirral, ending with breakfast at the end of the walk.

4   London Clarion Cyclists Club House at Nazeing in Essex

As the popularity of cycling and socialism grew, the Clarion Cycling Clubs spread throughout the country after 1900, including to London and the Home Counties. The Romford Clarion Club organized a camp in June 1910 so successfully that the London Clarion cyclists decided the establish a clubhouse of their own. The appeal of personal freedom through cycling, combined with the 'good fellowship' of belonging to a club, persisted. To have a clubhouse was an added appeal, and the London Clarions finally obtained their own in1913 at Broadley Common, near Nazeing on the Essex coast. It soon became the rural base for the London Clarions Fellowship, and continued to be used throughout the war-years and into the 1920s.[19]

The clubhouse could be reached from London after a full days cycling, and the members would have arrived in the evening tired and looking forward to their stay. Those for whom a bike ride as too long travelled by motor-bike or train. It was in quite an isolated location, but this was part of the appeal, with the orchard, kitchen garden and a triangular-shaped field where vegetables were grown. There was a also a large barn converted for dances, a shed housing a billiard table, dining-room, reading-room and a kitchen. It was run on co-operative lines, and by 1914 members were contributing 2/6 for an equal share. A report in the *Clarion* captured some of the enthusiasm:

…the members and visitors are Clarionettes with the usual amount of cheerfulness and sense of responsibility and a determination to get as much out of life as possible. For the London Clarion Club House is in the making and everyone knows that a clubhouse in the making is the happiest, jolliest, cheeriest kind of place that one can go to. The house at Broadley Common is in a good position for scenery and there are plenty of interesting beauty spots within an easy ride. When these are reached, and the cyclists are exhausted, they can return to the beauties of the clubhouse and be sure of good food and entertainment at their hands.20

These Clarion clubhouses for cyclists were eventually found all over the country, as cycling became even more popular and club membership increased. The bikes became cheaper to buy, both new and second-hand, and were easy and cheap to maintain as the early machines were basic and unsophisticated. From the start touring was popular, and parents more willing to allow their daughters to go on weekend jaunts with other girls in the group, to pre-planned destinations they knew in advance.

Many members of the NCCC were also members of the ILP and joined the Labour Party when it was formed in 1900.After 1929 cycling became more politically focused in response to the economic conditions, as well as threats from motor traffic and the new road lobbies. This political focus drew on the connection between the cheapness of cycling and its importance in the lives of the working class.21 The increasing encroachment of commercial and industrial development in the countryside was seen by many, not only socialists, as a tremendous threat to the amenities it offered and its 'purity'. The considerable emotional investment by socialists in the ideal world of natural landscape and 'wilderness' naturally meant they were inclined to be more militant in their opposition to the perceived threats.

The 1930s saw the erection of electricity pylons, the construction of new arterial roads, transport cafes, roadhouses and new housing developments spreading out from the suburbs into the countryside. Car-ownership was growing rapidly and owners often antagonistic to cyclists, trying at times to get them banned from main roads. To socialist cyclists it seemed as if the more prosperous middle-class, who could afford these vehicles, seemed intent on persecuting a great working-class pastime.[22]The large increase in motorized traffic was found not only on main roads, but on the minor ones and lanes previously the preserve of farm vehicles, livestock, cyclists and hikers. This appeared to many cyclists, ramblers and others as a threat to their rural idylls, and re-energized their enthusiasm for their activity or sport.

This new radicalism among cycling socialists saw a revival in the 1930s of Clarion Cycling Club membership, and many other left-wing groups such as the communist Red Wheelers Club in London. They were all anti-motoring, while the motoring organizations seemed to regard them as a threat to their investment in transport.[23]The Clarion cyclists saw motorists as the latest capitalist assault on the interests of the working-class, so defending cycling seemed part of a single cause. The suggestion was even made in *Clarion Cyclists* that disused railway tracks could be used as high speed roads, as a way of confining the anti-social car and reducing the damage it did.[24]

This contempt for motorized transport and its promoters in the press, such as the motoring correspondents, was echoed by several writers on the left. These motoring journalists seemed to act like agents for the car industry, and the *Observer's* seemed like ' a man who obviously loves the English countryside....yet drives his car up and down and round the counties of England, until no lane is safe from from his molestation, no villages unvisited by his peripatetic mechanisms. And week by week he divulges in the *Observer* carefully, charmingly, the result of his depredations, devoting all his considerable powers of persuasion to the task of inducing others to follow in his train'.[25]

The rejuvenation of the Clarion Cycling Club in the 1930s with a wider range of activities enabled it to expand on its mission of promoting the pleasures of cycling with good fellowship, mutual aid and promotion of the socialist message. The circulation of the *Clarion Cyclist* reached 5,575 in November 1936, and the wider remit of the club led it to arrange educational classes, set up more club houses with sleeping accommodation for touring groups, in addition to many activities, conferences, exhibitions and competitions. As a result the membership increased to 8,306 in 1936, when it became affiliated to the National Workers Sports Association. The founding of the Youth Hostels Association helped to facilitate longer tours, and groups of cyclists would also take advantage of the railways to book excursions, take groups to some distant station in the countryside and return home from another station.

As the urban working-class were cut off from the countryside, so the landscape and access to it became an important part of socialist political faith. This access took various forms, but cycling remained a constant and popular means of reaching the otherwise inaccessible un-spoilt areas of greatest scenic beauty. Most Clarion cyclists, Field Club members, and those in other socialist groups like the Labour League of Youth, chose their destinations with care hoping to reach the more remote areas, and become more acquainted with the 'wilder' places. In addition, they were meant to 'diffuse a love and knowledge of the animal and plant life and the fields', as well as 'protecting animals and birds, and preserving the commons and footpaths.' A socialist ideal of comradeship combined with fresh-air.26

The group cycle tours provided a camaraderie in the fraternal friendship of like-minded people, enjoying the exercise and open air. This sense of togetherness and fraternity in depressed economic times helps explain the delight in cycling, freed temporarily from the constraints of daily lives spent in office, factory, school or the dole-queue. It was leisure with a purpose, a simple past time spent in a healthy environment. By the1930s it no longer involved socialist missionary work among the rural population, but cycling still retained for many socialists a way of combining speed, fresh air, and a means of escape. It enabled them to discover the beauty of the countryside for a day or perhaps longer, before cycling back to city or town refreshed and re-energized for the week and work ahead.

3. FOLK ARTS, GARDENS, EDUCATION AND SCHOOLS

One of the ways in which socialists expressed the idealization of the countryside and rural life was through the rediscovery and revival of folk arts. This process started with the ethical socialists in the 1890s, their belief in a golden age of 'Merrie' England where an indigenous 'people's art' flourished. The folk revival continued in the 1900s and into the inter-war period, evolving and updating as it did so. William Morris and his followers imagined a pre-industrial age of superior social conditions and values, a world in which craftsmen could practice their skills unimpeded by capitalist profit-making and mass production. It was also a society in which the arts flourished – painting, music, song and dance – without the corrupting influence of commercialization, an authentic culture by and for the people.

It was a rural society made up of villages and small market towns, and in Robert Blatchford's *Merrie England* there is a constant contrast made between the dirt and squalor of industrial towns and the bucolic pleasures of Surrey, Suffolk and Hampshire:

> In the latter counties you will breath pure air, bright skies, clear rivers, clean streets and beautiful fields, woods and gardens; you will get cattle and streams and birds and flowers, and you know all these things are well worth having, and that none of them can exist side by side with the factory system….To make wealth for themselves they (the capitalists) destroy the beauty and health of your dwelling places; and then they sit in their suburban villas or on the hills and terraces of the lovely southern counties, and sneer at the "sentimentality" of the men who ask you to cherish beauty and to prize health.1

This was a far cry from the backstreets of Bradford and Manchester which had been so influential on the young Blatchford in shaping his political outlook. He had done so much to expose the iniquities of these places, but the desire to escape was always there, and eventually he was able to leave Manchester himself when the *Clarion* office moved to London. Blatchford later lived in London, and then moved to rural Norfolk, and eventually settled in Sussex tending his roses while criticizing the Labour Party and its leader. He saw nothing incompatible between being a socialist and living contentedly with the quiet rhythms of a country town, even if he was increasingly consumed by pastoral nostalgia and patriotism.

In an ideal rural society people would be self-sufficient and work far fewer hours than in factory production. Whether working as farmers or skilled craftsmen they would be self-employed and independent. Plain-living, high-thinking, simplicity and refinement were the ideals of ethical socialists which extended to clothing, furniture, diet, as well as spiritual and intellectual pleasures. The people would produce their own food, clothing, shelter and fuel, still with ample free time to pursue cultural, educational or outdoor interests. With the right guidance a whole new world would be opened up for the them:

> There are such pleasures as walking, rowing, swimming, football and cricket. There are the arts and drama. There are the beauties of nature. There is travel and adventure. Mere word cannot convey an idea of the intensity of these pleasures, Music alone is more delightful and more precious than all the vanities that wealth can buy, or all the carnal luxuries that folly can desire. The variety of pure and healthy pleasures are infinite.2

This re-awakening involved a rediscovery of rural folk arts including singing, dancing, local customs, festival and traditions. These often took place in the open air, such as dancing around the Maypole or Morris dancing. May Day had a special significance, not only as an ancient country rite of spring, but as the national day of labour, which connected the latter to the folk tradition. The May Pole was a significant symbol of the time, and many people looked forward to seeing them erected all over the country each year with "the boys and girls, young men and maidens, all joining in the mirth and folly of May Day."3The renewal of spring was made politically explicit, as in ILP May Day rallies where it was used to symbolize the better quality of life supposedly enjoyed by the workers in a rural golden age. Whether accurate or not, this was a powerful propaganda tool that enabled socialists to compare what they saw as the more satisfying life of the past compared with the tawdry materialism of the present.4 In his May Day speech of 1923, Ramsay MacDonald made this clear when he stated that socialism led to a renewal of life that would come "like the Spring everywhere – in the sky, in the fields, in the woods."[5]

·A·GARLAND·FOR·MAY·DAY·1895·
· DEDICATED·TO·THE·WORKERS·BY·WALTER·CRANE ·

5 'A Garland for May Day 1895 by Walter Crane

Folk-dancing and music became part of the programme of events at socialist gatherings, such as those organized by Fabian summer schools. Morris dancing had almost become extinct when Cecil Sharp saw it performed to the accompaniment of a concertina at Headington Quarry in December 1899. Sharp, then a Fabian socialist, began taking an interest in native folk song, and in researching the traditional and instrumental folk music of Britain. He hoped to spark a revival in interest which might lead to people re-engaging with the dances and songs of their region, preferably sung in local dialect. He believed these were a living cultural depository that placed the working man within an authentic native tradition of rural art, uncontaminated by middle class or commercial interference.

Sharp began seriously collecting songs in 1903 after visiting a friend in Somerset, eventually amassing 1600 tunes from over 350 local singers. In 1907 he published his *Morris Books*, and used examples from it in his illustrated lectures to encourage interest on the progressive Left. He extended the collecting to other counties, and also published *The Sword Dances of Northern England* in three volumes, including the Rapper Sword Dance from Northumberland and the Long Sword Dance from Yorkshire which led to a revival of these two traditional forms.6

These were presented as a new people's art, pure and unexploited by commerce, a spontaneous result of local people making their own entertainment. It was seen as a sign of a localism, and fraternal fellowship, that was genuinely authentic. Sharp also published song-books for use by teachers and children in the school music curriculum. The traditional words were accompanied by his own compositions, even though the originals would have been unaccompanied. The songbooks helped to disseminate and popularize English folksong in particular, and led to a vogue for it among some progressive people, although they were often more middle-class than Sharp would have liked.7

The Workers Educational Association also took up the cause, and began encouraging folk singing in their local branch activities and classes. The hope was that it would show the urban industrial worker how a vigorous working-class culture once existed and thrived in the countryside. Its advantage to socialism as an art form was that it allowed for the mass participation of people, and could involve their collective effort even though they had no previous training. Folk arts also evoked the countryside and rural scenes, and fitted easily into the idealized rural world so valued in the British socialist tradition.

Many traditional folk songs were sung as solo performances although often with accompanying choruses. These were usually repeated between verses, allowing for a form of mass participation. There were also opportunities for learning to play the instruments that accompanied the folk songs and dances, such as violin, pipes, flutes. In addition there was the chance to join a dance group, learning the dances and performing them. Finally there was the audience who participated not only by listening, often in the open air, but by joining in the choruses. The hope was that this could help put the urban working class back in touch with traditional rural culture by participating in one way or another, but not just as part of a passive 'consumer' audience at commercial bourgeois concerts. This helps explain the popularity of traditional folk song and dance for the early socialists, making them part of the "naturally educated men able to produce beautiful things."8

There was to be a reaction later against this kind of activity on grounds of its alleged inauthenticity, particularly the songs collected by Sharp and even his motivation. It was later often ridiculed and satirized, as in Kingley Amis's 1958 novel *Lucky Jim*, in which the head of the History department in a provincial university and his wife are lampooned as enthusiastic folk dancers. To some there seemed something bogus middle-class city dwellers dressing up as Morris men, and performing in their spare time as a hobby. But at the time it was a genuine attempt to revive the rural arts, and to try connecting them with the urban working class.9

Sharp's work inspired a vogue for collecting traditional song and dance that influenced others, notably the composer and socialist Ralph Vaughan Williams. He had a deep compassion for the dispossessed urban working classes, and a belief in the need for their spiritual and cultural elevation as well as material progress. Vaughan Williams collected his first song *Bushes and Brambles* at Ingrave in Essex in December 1903, and went on to collect over 800 songs mainly from Essex, Norfolk, and Sussex. He regarded folk songs as the expression of the cultural aspiration of the rural working-class, and as such the authentic voice of the people. He saw it as an important element in the national identity, and part of his mission as an English composer to promote it.10

The urge to revive and preserve traditional crafts of the countryside was inspired by the ideas of Ruskin and Morris, and found expression in the Home Arts and Industries Association. This was founded in 1884 with the primary aim of reviving the flagging skills of rural craftsmanship, threatened by mechanical production and increased urbanization. There was a belief that flourishing traditional crafts would help sustain rural communities and provide more satisfying work for country people than factory drudgery, with the added bonus that it would also prevent country folk from migrating to the cities to find work.

The HAIA had at its peak around 40 branches and 320 members spread around the country. In 1913 it held 200 classes and had 5,000 students attending. They were taught a wide range of handicrafts that included carpentry, wood carving, inlaying and veneering, wrought iron work, hand-beaten silver work, basket-weaving, hand-weaving and spinning. The classes were organized locally with usually unpaid volunteers as instructors, and an annual exhibition was held at the Albert Hall in London to display the best of the work.11

The socialist sympathizer and architect C.R. Ashbee was an early advocate of reviving the Guild idea for preserving and encouraging traditional craft skills. He opened the Guild and School of Handicrafts at Toynbee Hall in the East End of London in June 1888. It was such a success that it had to move to larger premises at Essex House in the Mile End Road, where the Guild carried out carpentry, carving, cabinet-making and decorative painting. A blacksmiths shop was built in the garden, and metalwork, silverwork and jewellery-making were added to the Guild trades. There were a growing number of commissions, with Ashbee's own architectural practice among the main customers for furniture, as well as the wealthy patrons of the Toynbee Hall settlement. There was a lively social life among the Guild members, who would cycle down to the country and stay in a series of cottages for weekend breaks and holidays. Ashbee had tried to engage the interest of William Morris in the enterprise, and was 'going to forge a weapon for you; and thus I too work for you in the overthrow of society', but Morris but was too involved in his own projects for revolutionary socialism at the time to take much interest.12

In 1901 with the expiry of the lease on Essex House, the Guild of Handicrafts started to look for new premises that were suitable for the pursuit of 'good honest craftsmanship.' Ashbee decided to look at properties in the country, and various places were inspected before he discovered Chipping Campden in the Cotswolds. It was rather sleepy and run-down but Ashbee was impressed with the picturesque nature and the authenticity of the place, with its honey-coloured stone and medieval atmosphere. A 'democratic' decision was made after the foremen of the various departments of the Guild visited, and a majority voted in favour of relocating. On hearing of the vote by 2 to 1, Ashbee wrote that he was 'glad to think that the men themselves have decided on the whole it is better to leave Babylon to go home to the land'.13It seemed as if he had found his 'City of the Sun', and 150 East Enders decamped to the quiet of the Cotswolds and occupied the Old Silk Mill, soon to be renamed Essex House. They acquired presses from Kelmscot House on William Morris's death, and had drawing offices and showrooms on the ground floor, jewellery workshops on the second, and carpentry workshop on the top floor, with a blacksmiths workshop in the yard. Being in the country was like going back to first principles for Ashbee, for apart from his romantic socialist feeling for the countryside, he also had a special sympathy for Nature and natural forms, and spoke of 'going home' to the land.14

Ashbee thought it was in the country that native craftsmanship could flourish in an environment unencumbered with too many commercial concerns. And for a time the Guild continued with its success, and soon became integrated into the life of the local village community. Local craftsmen were employed to fill vacancies, and paid more than the local wages. Regular plays and classes were put on, which the locals were allowed to attend, in cooking, woodcraft, gardening, music and keep-fit. Some very fine work was produced, including jewellery, cabinet-making, and silverwork, but the competition was increasing from mass produced products, particularly machine-made replicas, and within a few years the Guild was facing bankruptcy and closed in 1905.15

In 1911 a new vicar was appointed to the parish of Thaxted in Essex who had a different concept of community in mind when he took up his appointment in 1911. Conrad Noel was on a mission to spread the social gospel, and create a progressive socialist community in the process. Noel was a Christian socialist, and his appointment in the gift of Lady Warwick who had high hopes for his missionary experiment. He began by making the beautiful parish church at Thaxted the center of the whole community, but soon looked for other means of reaching the wider local population. His wife Miriam persuaded him to allow her to organize classes in country-dancing for the young people. At first Noel was doubtful, as he did not want to encourage an artificial folk revival for its own sake, but he came to see that traditional dance and song could help to express and encourage a popular feeling for a new world of fellowship and unity.

A tradition of local Morris dancing remained intact in that part of Essex, and so lessons began in country dancing and old local songs. A teacher was hired to conduct the classes, and they proved so popular that Miriam Noel was trained to carry on the teaching. The result was a genuine revival of local song and dance among the villagers, and the tunes could he heard everywhere with old melodies being whistled and sang in the fields, pubs, and workplaces. In the summer of 1911 a team of dancers from Thaxted performed in Cambridge, at the local flower show, and at Easton Lodge at the invitation of Lady Warwick. Noel also encouraged other community groups including a revival of the Thaxted Scout troop, which quickly grew in numbers. They went on all the usual scouting excursions, including camps and other outdoor forms of self-reliance. All this local activity was intended to encourage a sense of fellowship, and a grass-roots socialism based on traditional customs and values.[16]

In 1914 the composer Gustav Holst visited Thaxted and was impressed with the Tudor atmosphere of the village, the handsome Guildhall building and the immensity of the Church, as well as with the socialist community that Noel was pioneering. He decided to rent a thatched cottage in Monk Street and stay for the summer which he continued to do for several years. Holst was left-leaning, if not as far as Noel himself, but soon got involved in the musical life of the community. He coached the choir and for the 1916 Festival supplemented it with choirs from St Paul's Girls School in London and Morley College, both at which he taught. They sang in the church which was full of wild flowers, in the fields, and in people's houses for 15 hours a day. It seemed that music-making and socialism come together in this place naturally, with the whole community involved in choral work, or folk music and Morris dancing.[17]

The idea of learning crafts, skills and self-reliance in the open air was the main objective of the Woodcraft Folk movement, which in its early years had a strong co-operative and anti-capitalist flavor. It was started by Leslie Paul in February 1925 at Lewisham in south-east London with a small groups that had broken away from the Scouting and Guide movement. It grew rapidly, and by December 1925 had about70 members mainly in the south London area, but by 1929 the membership was in the thousands.

Leslie Paul was a socialist who emphasized 'tribal training' as a central activity for the young which involved camping and open air activities such as rambling and hiking. He saw these as important elements of youth training and character-building, the aim of which was to counter the malign influences of capitalism. The group camp, for example, provided an education in the daily practicalities of co-operative living which involved everybody in cooking, washing-up and cleaning. This shared social endeavor was seen as a contrast to the selfish individualism of an acquisitive society, and aimed to combat it in this way.

In all the outdoor activity of the Woodcraft Folk there was an implied antipathy to commerce, competitive individualism and conventional education. Being closer to nature, respecting the environment and living co-operatively would "lift young people out of the apathy of civilization." Communal living or 'tribalism,' would "present the boy with a form of organization he can understand and enjoy. The simple government of the gang invites this particularly and the ideal of service to his fellows is first learnt in the realization of his duty to the gang"[18]

The Woodcraft Folk were strongly influenced by the personal philosophies of Paul and John Hargrave, who had earlier founded the Kibbo Kift, a similar break-away group from the Boy Scouts. Initially there was a good deal of tribal and mystical references, as part of the reverence for the outdoors and the natural world. For a time Woodcraft Folk was overtly socialist in orientation, overlaid with mystical romanticism and a nostalgia for pre-industrial times. Paul felt they were leading the way towards creating a "new world order" in which the worker would be "emancipated from wage slavery and given economic power"[19] This mixture of naivety and grandiosity seems far-fetched to modern minds, especially as the means to this utopia were a few thousand girls and boys based in south London. But the idealism, driven by strong anti-capitalist ideology, was a link to William Morris and the utopian socialism of the late nineteenth century.[20]

At first the Woodcraft Folk had close links with the Royal Arsenal Cooperative Society, but the Co-operative Union was slow to accord it official recognition, and by 1938 all links had been broken. They also remained isolated from other socialist groups, despite having a lot in common with some of them. This may have been because others had their own youth groups, and they had little in common with each other. But the Woodcraft Folk were seen by some on the Left as the acceptable face of scouting, even though they retained elements of the scouting movement that some socialists disdained. Yet they can be seen as part of the inter-war process by which youth outdoor activity became increasingly politicized across the ideological spectrum, and at the same time appealing to young people with its ceremonies, rituals and adventure training.[21]

Preparing for Breakfast.

6 Woodcraft Folk Camp in the late 1920s

The outdoor activities of the Woodcraft Folk - camping, trekking, hiking and so on – were often quite strenuous. At Easter 1927, for example, hikes started at 7am each day with a warning that "laggards will be left behind". Pageantry, ceremony, and songs were vital elements in keeping the children interested, but always in the form of active recreation rather than passive amusement. There were also lessons on World History and Human Evolution, which Paul saw as essential in developing the mind and in giving a 'correct' historical perspective. He argued that "man does not live by bread alone but is a creature of music, art, and dancing and poetry from which a touch of the cosmic is appropriate."[22]

All Woodcraft Folk activity was based on the principle of 'learning by doing' to shape the primal instincts of children and turn them into productive citizens:

> ...if the race is to survive, we need to produce men and women who by their knowledge, their physical fitness and mental independence, shall bring qualities, quick brains and boundless vitality to bear on man's struggle for liberty. We are the revolution, with the health that is ours and with the intellect and physique that will be the heritage of those we train, we are paving the way for that reorganization of the economic system which will make the rebirth of the human race.23

There was a great deal along similar lines in Woodcraft literature with an emphasis on working-class heroes of the past, the aim to give working-class children a sense of their hidden history. But Paul insisted that this had to be achieved mainly in the open air not in the classroom, with a constant communing with nature. It also meant recreating living like a 'primitive tribe' so their essential vitality could be replicated. At every meeting the formal greeting and assent was 'How', and on some camps the children would live in tepees and sing "Who are the Folks?" including the chorus "Hark the beating of our tom-toms. See the fire before our wig-wam" The children were attracted by these exotic rituals, the outdoor life, colourful pageantry, camp fire singing, nature rambles, hiking, and so on.24

We have already seen the importance of 'the garden' in the mythology and iconography of early English socialist thinking, and in the illustrations of Walter Crane and Edward Burne Jones. The garden, and exposure to the natural world in it, also played a part in the work of educational progressives who had socialist sympathies. From the 1890s a few such educational reformers were concerned with making the child the centre of the school experience, but also ensuring they had access to a healthy natural open air environment.

These pioneers believed that the learning environment should adapt to the needs of the child, rather than the child fitting into a rigid system whether natural or constructed, and the garden allowed the child to relate to other living things, and through this to the wider community and society. The keys to education were curiosity, and self-discovery, not rote-learning or the grad-grind methods so much favoured by Victorian schools. This belief motivated many of those concerned with the education of working-class children, but also those who wanted to liberate middle-class children from stultifying ethos of the public schools and their values.

The pioneer of nursery education was Margaret McMillan, who always emphasized the connection between a child's physical environment and its intellectual development. Margaret was converted to Christian Socialism by her sister Rachel after moving from Edinburgh to London in 1888. They both worked in homes for young girls, attended socialist meetings, meeting Morris, H.M. Hyndman, Ben Tillet and other leading figures on the Left. The sisters began giving evening classes to working-class girls, and helped strikers in the London Dockers strike of 1889, hoping to spread the Christian Socialist message to the workers.25

 In 1892 they moved to Bradford, an early centre of socialist activity, and from this base were involved in spreading the socialist gospel throughout the North of England, joining the Labour Church, the Fabian Society and the ILP soon after it was founded in 1893. Margaret became interested in working with slum children in Bradford, and tried to improve their physical and educational well-being. Together with the school medical officer of health, Dr. James Kerr, she carried out the first survey of the medical health of elementary school children in Britain. This revealed the extent of ill-health and malnutrition, and the pair campaigned to improve conditions in the schools, and for the provision of free school meals. This campaign was eventually successful when the Schools Meals Act was passed in 1906 by which the state accepted responsibility for the good nourishment as well as the education of all children.

On returning to London, Margaret and Rachel became involved in setting up the first school clinic at Bow in 1908, then one in Deptford in1910 to serve schools in that area. They went on to found three so-called 'Night Camps' for babies and children for slum children to rest, bath and receive extra education. While exploring a property that had been donated for one of these camps, Margaret discovered a garden which she realized could do so much to enhance the lives of poor children:

An elder tree that had leaned, black and dismal against the wall all winter suddenly put on afresh new dress of green, which after a few days, when we had white-washed the walls and paling around it, looked perfectly dazzling. And on either side of it (divided by only a few palings) are the friendliest kind kind of garden. On the right the low wall is covered by a splendid vine which yields many clusters of grapes in autumn – huge grapes they might be if we could build a hothouse around them. The vine would throw its wide loving loving arms over the wall....26

In some of the worst conditions found anywhere in Europe the garden could provide an oasis of beauty, and have a transformative effect on children deprived of sunlight and that beauty in their lives. McMillan thought that nursery schools should be designed to meet children's needs and longings, and encourage their imagination and creativity. In the school garden this could be "expressed in everything - in the low fencing and little gates, the open gables through which a screen of June leaves rustle."27

In 1914, the McMillan sisters started an open-air nursery in Deptford based on their educational principles, which soon had thirty children ranging in age from seven months to seven years. In addition they started a college to train nursery teachers in the methods they pioneered. There were more publications, notably *Nursery Education* of 1919, in which Margaret elaborated the importance of the outdoors in pre-school education. It argued that children were healthier if they were allowed to play and learn in the open-air, and allowed to explore ways in which nature could be used to help them learn. The school garden was vital in this and should be planned to meet the needs and wishes of the children, not treated as an outdoor gymnasium for climbing and running about although these had their value, but for the children to be stimulated with the sight, smell, and sounds of lovely and strange things.28

If possible, there should always be trees for climbing, to provide shelter on wet weather, and shade on sunny days:

In the spring and summer their stillness, their movement, their streaming beauty, have a strange kind of reassuring effect even on the youngest...the plain trees days...Poplars, limes, sycamores, some chestnuts (but the chestnuts do not like smoke), hardy willows, weeping birches, and even ash and oak...Even flowering trees do well (ours yields no fruit). The garden is very gay in April and May, climbing roses do not count among other trees as such. They grow riotously in spite of fumes in south east London, covering arches and pillars...29

The importance of trees also applied to flowers, and the children's garden should be planned so it displayed interest throughout the year. The children could then see laurel, holly and jasmine in December, snow drops and crocuses in February, and sweeps of bulbs in March, before cherry blossom appeared in May. In this way the child would get a real sense of the changing seasons reflected in plants and flowers:

> It is a question of getting the garden ideas to replace the fixed idea of indoor things, cut flowers and bulbs in pots, and little boxes of flowers – all good in their way but giving no adequate impressions to the child of the real nature of living colour. 30

Although McMillan thought there was no substitute for seeing 'real' nature, the school garden was a long way from the 'wild' places admired by outdoor socialists in a different context. But the children of the city slums had no chance of seeing these kind of places, or any scenery in its natural habitat. To have a garden as part of the school meant the children could see, experience, and identify all the flowers, shrubs and trees every day. Their senses would be re-awakened by perfumes and textures, and help to fix lasting memories. The very young loved to smell the perfume of flowers, and even when they could only speak a little, perhaps at three, could be encouraged to describe what they saw and experienced.

Every nursery school, McMillan believed, should also have a herb garden with all the wonderful smells of marjoram, mint, and thyme among others, while the children could press the leaves and smell their fingers. A kitchen garden also enabled a city child to learn about shape and colour, as well as the feel of different vegetables and fruits, see them grow and taste them raw. They could sow seeds and see potatoes, beetroots, carrots, raspberries and blackcurrants growing, all to be associated for them with warm summer days in their memory banks. Ideally a nursery school should be located near a river, so the children could see the moving water, and the changing of the river as the seasons change.31

The school garden should also have plenty of natural objects such as stones, rocks and trees which should provide plenty of opportunity for climbing and jumping. It should be possible for children to learn about the wildlife that is attracted into any garden, particularly bird-life, insects and pond-life. They should be encouraged to turn up stones to find insects underneath, learn about animals and develop an empathy for them. It might also be possible for them to keep their own rabbits and hens as well as fish in a pond.32

These were radical ideas for the time, and intended to bring the countryside into the town by simulating a natural environment the children could enjoy. But McMillan also believed children should be taken into the real countryside whenever possible, or even to the seaside. For poor urban children of the time holidays were an unknown luxury, partly due to lack of paid holidays for their parents. The school holidays were difficult time for both children and parents, if they did not live close to a municipal park it meant playing in the streets all day, on the landings of their tenement buildings, or in confined backyards.

For their own nursery children the McMillan's was able to organize annual trips into the country only because a sympathetic benefactor provided the means. In 1924 a Miss Hawtrey invited the children from Deptford to spend the summer holidays in her big house at Avery Hill in Kent, later the site of Margaret McMillan College. This experiment was repeated in 1925, and in the following year at Lady Warwick's estate at Easton Lodge. For the children this experience of the countryside had a liberating effect, and it was noted by Margaret how much of what they had learned in the classroom and garden sprang to life there with the guidance of their teachers.

They saw more types of tree growing in woodland, fruits growing naturally in the hedgerows, and for the first time wildlife like herons and ducks, deer grazing and all the smells of the countryside. This more authentic experience was clearly preferable to a little urban garden, as their while life would be if it could be spent wholly in the country. But these summer trips gave them a glimpse of another world, more fulfilling than the urban life to which they all had to return and spend the rest of their lives. At least during the brief years of their childhood they should have the chance whenever possible to to free their natural vitality:

England is full of beautiful houses, surrounded by scenes of unrivalled beauty and great expanses. The homes are passing out of the hands of ancestral owners;

but every normal person must hope and desire that the beauty will never pass away, never be lost, never be desecrated. I think there is only one sure way of preserving it . In the receptive years, in childhood, all should learn to *love* this beauty, to wonder at and treasure it as a gift of unseen and beneficent powers, and this they can do by beholding it, and living in it with real helpers and teachers for at least a few weeks, until at last in becomes a sacred heritage.33

The value of open air education was taken up by several local authorities before 1918, notably the socialist-controlled London County Council. It set up the Bostall Wood Open Air School in 1908 in order to take tubercular children out of their poor housing environment and provide a healthy one to aid their recovery. Several other local authorities, such as Birmingham and Leicester, did the same. By 1911 there were nine such schools and, as the results were remarkable with healthier children putting on weight, the process continued after 1918 so that by 1937 there were 155 schools catering for 16,500 children.34 They generally took every opportunity to access the open air with classrooms as open as possible, preferably on three sides while on the fourth there was a blackboard and cupboard space.

The teacher, socialist, and Labour Party activist Leah Manning assumed the headship of an open air in Cambridge in 1918. She had been a teacher at another Cambridge school in a poor district, and was appalled by the malnutrition and living conditions of her pupils. She was delighted to take charge at Vine Road Open Air School which the local authority had created when it took over an old farm just outside the city. Leah largely agreed with the philosophy of the McMillan's, and she was determined to make Vine Road work for the benefit of the mainly poor children who were sent there. Her motives were not merely to improve the health of the children, but to improve their lives and life chances by experiencing nature in an educational environment they would not otherwise have done. She was to remain there for twenty years until elected, briefly, as the Labour MP for Islington East in February 1931.

Another socialist educationalist who attempted to put his ideals into practice was Edward Lowerison, who also believed that outdoor activities would help to counteract the growing divorce of knowledge from the physical environment. A well-known lecturer on the socialist circuit and a Fabian Society National Executive member, he had been the founder of several Clarion Field Clubs and was a frequent contributor to the *Clarion* paper. As a teacher in the East End of London he had helped to set up the London Schools Swimming Association, and had prevailed on the Fabian Society to provide a trophy for the LSSA annual championships, which were reported in the Fabian News.35 Lowerison also attempted to set up a London Schools Rambler's Association in the hope it would increase children's appreciation of their natural environment, and provide teachers with a 'medium of exchange of botany and natural insect specimens, fossils etc, and facilitate what is more important – the exchange of idea with regard to Nature education and methods and appliances.'36

In 1899, after he was dismissed from his teaching post in Hackney for writing letters to the socialist press, Lowerison decided to set up his own school to put his ideals into practice. He had already outlined these ideas in the *Clarion* with a series of articles titled 'My Ideal School,' in which the laws of health and exercise would be taught, the principles of justice and gentleness and also draw from each child their natural abilities with a focus on reasoning.37 These articles created considerable interest and led to a meeting at the vicarage of Cartmel Robinson on 16 December 1899, where a plan was drawn up to create the school. There were donations made by *Clarion* readers in shares of 10 shillings each guaranteed by the paper, and a committee elected.

The Ruskin Home School was initially located at Hunstanton in Norfolk, but in 1902 it moved to larger premises near Heacham. Many donations were received for the new premises including natural history specimens, bees, chickens and even a pony. The aim from the outset was to de-institutionalize education as much as possible, with more self-discovery and self-learning, experience - based education which took advantage of the local countryside, the lanes, fields, and rivers. Lowerison, like McMillan, opposed what they thought was the drift to specialization, and wanted children to appreciate the unity and inter-connectivity of knowledge. The amount of time spent in the classroom was limited, and children were allowed out into the open air as much as possible, so the Ruskin School timetable was organized to allow the afternoons to be free for cycling, walking about and other outdoor activities.38

There was a debate among early socialist educational reformers about the role of physical exercises or drills, and also of competitive sport and team games. Lowerison was quite relaxed about the nature of the physical activity at Ruskin so long as it was outdoors. There were team games like cricket and football, but he thought that children derived more benefit from physical activities that were not competitive or based on teams, and swimming, cycling and walking were undertaken for personal pleasure rather than competition. The school was deliberately located in the Norfolk countryside as Lowerison believed children would be more likely to thrive than if confined in large towns, and could be at their most natural when playing, running, cycling, or almost any fresh-air activity.39

RUSKIN SCHOOL HOME.
Heacham-on-Sea Norfolk.

7   Ruskin School Home pupils at the Boathouse.

The emphasis in the curriculum at Ruskin Home School was on learning about the natural world, and children were permitted to keep animals, nature diaries, collect fossils and pre-historic lint implements round around the countryside on their afternoon expeditions. They had their boat and were responsible for looking after it in a boatshed, and the school had its own museum to display objects found and even donated some to the British Museum and elsewhere. This was all in tune with learning by discovery, something Lowerison shared with Margaret McMillan and other comrades, who despaired of the growing emphasis on book-based rote learning.40

The role of landscape and gardens were important in the schemes of other educationalists who wanted to break from the rigid hierarchy and conformity of the public schools. There were middle-class progressive parents who could afford to pay the fees at schools such as Abbotsholme, Bedales, Summerhill and Bryanston, all set in parks or rural landscapes. Though the founders of these schools saw themselves as 'progressives' rather than socialists, they did incorporate some ideas of William Morris, such as the teaching of crafts and art. A few were, however, on the left and shared with Margaret McMillan a belief in putting children at the center of the whole educational experience. They were also determinedly co-educational at a time when private and most state schools were single gender. The emphasis of the public schools on uniforms, prefects, muscular Christianity, the military ethos, patriotism, strict discipline, and a narrow curriculum based on classical languages, was rejected. Instead, they favored the encouragement of free-thinking, self-discovery, and the development of natural talent in the arts and sciences. They wanted the child to develop a questioning approach to everything, perhaps even the basis of society that itself that enabled them to enjoy their privileges.

These progressives shared the assumptions of the earlier socialists about the importance of the countryside and the natural environment, and the effect they had on character. The philosopher Bertrand Russell, and his wife Dora, set up Beacon Hill School in 1927, located in countryside near Petersfield in Hampshire. Both were socialists and pacifists, and Dora insisted on an idyllic rural environment for the new school. Their daughter Katherine later described the location as consisting of '200 acres of woods and valleys with deer and rabbits and stoats and weasels and huge yew trees we could into from higher trees and absolutely magnificent beech trees for climbing…'[41]

The aim of Beacon Hill was to educate the 'whole child' so creativity and self-expression were encouraged. The school was non-hierarchical and secular, with morality and reasoning developing 'from the child's actual experience in a democratic group.' This was helped by the children's access to the natural world in the grounds, and by learning to be at one with nature and to be integral to it. It was hoped in this way they would be able to understand easily about the processes of nature, to understand plant and animal life, and be inspired to creativity by its beauty. The opportunities for walking, swimming in the rivers and lakes, playing games in the grounds, and socializing in the open air would, the Russell's believed, lead to more positive character-building with a social purpose. The site on the South Downs was deliberately chosen to be well away from corrupting urban influences, as well as bureaucratic interference and inspection.42

The wealthy socialists, Leonard and Dorothy Elmhirst, purchased Dartington Hall in Devon in 1925, to create a progressive ecommunity. Although medieval in origin, the building was almost derelict when the Elmhirsts arrived to have them extensively renovated. Leonard had spent some years in India, where he was influenced by Rabindranath Tagore and his efforts to introduce education and rural reconstruction to local communities. They had been looking for some time for an ideal rural site to locate their own community experiment when they found Dartington Hall and estate near Dartmouth in south Devon, and it seemed ideal for their requirements. The plans involved not only a school, but also an arts centre to foster traditional and modern crafts, and a model farming community.

In the school there was a minimum of formal classroom teaching, and the children learnt by direct involvement in their environment as well as in the activities of a working country estate. Dorothy also wanted the school to be involved with child development from the earliest years, and a purpose built school for nursery education was opened between 1928-31.The beautiful gardens were recreated by Dorothy, including a tiltyard, the possible remains of what was once an Elizabethan water garden. Sculpture by some of the leading artists of the day, such as Henry Moore, were placed in the grounds to merge organically with the environment. Many new plant species were added, shrubs planted and magnificent lawns and vistas created. These were seen as essential elements in fostering the child's creativity amid such natural beauty.43

The first headmaster, W.B. Curry, was an enthusiastic proponent of modern educational theories and did his best with the staff to put Dorothy's ideas into practice. None of the usual public school features were tolerated, such as appointing prefects or hierarchies of any kind, and there was absolutely no trace of jingoism or militarism of any kind. At its peak, before and after the Second World War, Dartington Hall had several hundred pupils and was favoured by progressively-minded parents, usually well-off liberal-left or socialist parents, especially when the teaching became more formalized and the school acquired a high reputation for teaching in the arts. The assumption behind its idyllic garden was that the pursuit of knowledge separated from self-discovery and development was futile.

8 Dartington Hall and Gardens with a Henry Moore reclining figure

The basic philosophy at Dartington was that all of life should be part of the learning experience, and all experience was part of education. Being surrounded by beauty in the gardens and countryside was a daily reminder to the children and staff that the natural state of human beings was in a natural environment, a counter-point to urban distractions and pollution.44

The countryside therefore nourished people's intellectual and spiritual needs, and awakened those that had long remained dormant. The belief in this effect explains the almost reverential attitude to the country and its indigenous crafts and culture by many early socialists. The exile of the urban working class from the countryside, and their incarceration in unhealthy cities and towns, had prevented them fulfilling their potential as fully developed human beings. They had been cheated of their heritage, and finding the means to re-engage with it was a necessary preparation for a socialist future.

It was hoped that the revival of the folk arts and crafts, dancing, singing, drama, woodwork, and traditional customs would also help to re-establish the link between the past and present, and remind urban dwellers of their shared rural heritage. The garden can also be seen in this context as a way of releasing the natural curiosity and appreciation for nature that was believed to reside in all people, however long they had been cut off from their rural roots. The garden was a resource through which both adults and children could experience a spiritual refreshment, and even personal transformation. By learning to appreciate colour and form, in acquiring knowledge of flowers, plants, trees, and wild-life that they attracted, it was possible to become human in a full sense. The experience was part of a spiritual journey through which people would become whole again, dispelling the alienation and anomie of capitalist materialism and their urban lives. In an ideal world all adults and children would be able to benefit from this, but until society was re-arranged to provide for it, progressive experiments and organization would have to do the pioneering work, laying the ground for a better world to come.

4.C O-OPERATIVE COMMUNITIES AND LAND SETTLEMENTS

Some of those impatient for the arrival of a socialist society after 1890 sought to put their ideals into practice by setting up ideal rural communities or land colonies. There had always been a connection between socialism and communitarianism in England, and these latest communities were heirs to the Digger settlements of the seventeenth century. They shared a similar belief in the right of the people to have free access to common land, economic and social equality, and the close relationship between people and the land made closer by the need to work and live off it.

The founders of more recent land settlements were also inspired by a belief in honest toil, craftsmanship and self-sufficiency. This meant leaving modern commercial society behind, and attempting a personal salvation through a revolutionary change in lifestyle. In partnership with other like-minded people they hoped to find a New Jerusalem in which they could find this personal renewal. They may have looked backwards for much of their inspiration, but they were also looking forward to a different and better quality of life.

At a time when the possibilities of radical change in Britain was limited, these land colonists wanted to set an example and encourage others to set up similar ventures. These local utopian communities often thrived, and continued beyond 1918, as the prospect of social transformation through parliamentary means seemed increasingly unlikely. The Labour Party was intent on pursuing the parliamentary path to socialism, involving piecemeal improvement in the material conditions of the working class, but with less apparent interest in the spiritual transformation of their lives. The impatience among some utopian socialists with conventional Labour politics and trade union attitudes, fed into a desire for literally ploughing their own furrow.

Although the Labour Party seemed to be sidelining much of this radical idealism, it was still heir to the tradition of British radicalism that included the Co-operative and Chartist movements. The former aimed to share the profits from trade and land, while the latter sought to extend the franchise but also to set up village communities in the

the 1840s such as O'Connorville, Snigs End, Lowbands and Minster Lovell.1 But it was the influence of William Morris and John Ruskin who had most effect on the later land colonies, especially in their ideas about community-based co-operation, with traditional crafts practiced using local materials. Fear and loathing of industrialism and mass production was also strong, and linked to a vision of life which could lead to a kind of personal redemption, both cultural and economic.

Several of the early socialist community experiments were rooted in this tradition, including Edward Carpenter's group at Milnthorpe near Sheffield. Formed in the 1890s, Carpenter was concerned about creating a tolerant society of men and women where gender and sexual differences were tolerated, seeing socialism worked out in the daily livesof the community members. Carpenter was able to purchase the site with a family legacy and built a new house upon it. Soon after settling in he wrote describing his new rural utopia as consisting of 'about seven acres altogether; we are gardening about two acres, fruit, flowers and vegetables; about two and half acres grass and about the same quantity part wheat for ourselves and part oats for the horse…'2

In going back to the land, and retuning to nature, the Milnethorpe colony practiced vegetarianism, abstained from alcohol and smoking, as well as salt and drugs. It was abstemious in other respects also, particularly involving the food consumed and in dietary matters generally. In this sense they were pioneers, determined to resist the synthetic and unhealthy packaged for mass consumption. They practiced simple living but maintained high standards, helped perhaps by their relative isolation from the pressures of modern life. Carpenter became something of a guru, encouraging others to form similar settlements elsewhere, such the Norton colony formed in1896. The Milnethorpe settlement was highly successful and lasted over forty years before Carpenter and his companion, George Morrell, departed south for the warmer climes of Surrey.

During the 1890s the other experiments in communal living were also influenced by ideas of self-sufficiency and communal living. Robert Smith, a socialist printer from Manchester, was sufficiently impressed with Blatchford's description of living off the land that he set up a small community at Maryland in Essex in 1895. He acquired eleven acres and advertised for others with a similar interest in socialism and farming to join him and his family.4 They did so, but had a difficult start trying to find the best crops to grow and methods to use. After some experimentation they realized the micro-climate and soil in that part of Essex was best suited for market gardening. They had glasshouses constructed in which fruit and vegetables were grown using intensive methods of cultivation that eventually covered an enormous area.

The vast acreage of glasshouses was in addition to the cloches and sheds where the fruit and vegetables were packed, ready to send to market. It became almost an industrial process in the methods and intensity of production, rather in contrast to the self-sufficiency preached by Blatchford, to whom leisure was just as important as the work that sustained it. But the Maryland community showed that a small group of motivated people, working as one and sharing the load equally, was able to make a success of an enterprise. It certainly impressed Peter Kropotkin visited and wrote an introduction to the guidance manual Smith prepared for this kind of horticulture. The reputation of the colony spread and it received many other visitors, including Beatrice and Sidney Webb who were unconvinced.5

When George Lansbury visited he was impressed enough to persuade Joseph Fels, a millionaire American soap manufacturer and philanthropist, to purchase a larger site of almost 600 acres at Nipell's Farm nearby. It was intended to be run on the same co-operative lines, and to provide relief for the unemployed on a permanent basis. Fels divided the land into plots of between five or six acres, with houses and outbuildings on each one as well fruit trees for cultivation. Smith became the supervisor of the project, and the manager of 'Fel's Fruit Farm, Windmill Nurseries and French Gardens.' By this time a good deal of the early idealism of the Maryland settlers seems to have dissipated in their enthusiasm for more efficient production, although Smith personally remained loyal to his socialist principles. But the original ideal of self-sufficiency had clearly been breached with their business model, and the lack of an underlying set of agreed principles to guide the community. But still the business failed eventually because of the lack of good rail links to the London markets, and due to the smallness of the plots that made an adequate scale of production impossible.6

Another strong influence on these rural communities was Leon Tolstoy, as elements of his philosophy fitted in with English idealist socialism, including rejection private property and capitalism itself. His advocacy of the subsistence life based on personal labour fed into the English Digger tradition, and his advocacy of vegetarianism and abstinence from tobacco and alcohol with puritan radicalism. Tolstoy expounded on his views in *What I Believe* (1884), *What Shall We Do Then?* (1885), and *The Kingdom of God is Within You* (1889), also in his novels through the mouths of characters such as Levin in *Anna Kerenina* who at one point speaks as if with the author's thoughts:

> You know that capitalism opposes the workers. Our workmen, the peasants, bear the whole burden of labour, but are so placed that, work as they may, they cannot escape from their degrading position. All the profits of their labour, by which they might better their conditions, give themselves some leisure, and consequently gain some education, all this surplus value is taken away by the capitalists.

Tolstoy came to his views after a close reading of the gospels and the life of Jesus, but rejected organized religion and the state apparatus, seeking to turn away from mass society with all its corruption and distractions. To him the people should earn the essentials of life through labour in close contact with the soil, or what he termed 'bread labour'.7

An early covert to Tolstoyan ideas was J.C. Kenworthy, a socialist who had lived among the poor in London's Canning Town. For two years he had tried to establish local co-operative societies in collaboration with the Mansfield House University Settlement. This was an urban 'Mission', one of several established by Oxbridge colleges in the poorer areas of London, intended to give undergraduates the opportunity to work among the laboring poor, and hopefully develop a social conscience. These efforts to create people's co-operatives failed, but Kenworthy persisted with the idea that a socialist society could be started by re-organizing the trading relations between people. Together with a local clergyman, the Rev. J. Bruce Wallace, he set up the Brotherhood Trust, intended to be the core of a future Co-operative Commonwealth. In January 1894 it opened new premises as a grocery and vegetable co-operative aiming to pay trade union wage rates, old age pensions, and sickness benefits to members from the profits, and eventually to buy land for resettlement in the countryside.

Kenworthy was also influenced by Ruskin, Henry George and Herbert Mills who had started an 'industrial village' at Windermere to produce craft products, and by General Booth's colony at Hadleigh in Essex. Kenworthy elaborated his own form of Christian communal salvation:

> The part of our 'programme' which differentiates us from others who seek after the ideal society, is the determination that, let the world go in such a way as it pleases. We, each one at our own pace, for the salvation of our own soul, must live fraternally towards all men. That principle of conduct seemingly so individualistic, is really the basic principle of their Kingdom of Heaven which Jesus and all the prophets have foreseen.8

This did indicate the point of departure and difference between the idealistic communitarians and more ideological socialists. The former sought to withdraw from the rest of society, rejecting it as morally unacceptable and incapable of reforming itself, while they sought to create their own little utopias. The mainstream ideological socialist wanted the overthrow of capitalism, either by revolutionary means or by gaining parliamentary power. They thought a direct engagement with society was essential in this struggle, trying to convince the masses of their case and the need for radical reform. This helps to explain the antagonism to utopian communities in the socialist press, especially in the *Clarion* which, although itself opposed to parliamentary socialism, believed fervently in the need to convert the people to a 'purer' form socialism by education and propaganda. It had no time for utopian experiment, regarding them as irrelevant to the cause of creating socialism for all.

The Brotherhood Trust set up a co-operative in Croyden and published its own journal *The New Order*, full of adverts for their co-operative services such as grocery deliveries. This group soon broke up,and one faction led by Kenworthy set up a new settlement in February 1897 at Purleigh. It began with only five people, a house, two cottages, workshops, and an incubator, but it soon grew with more people joining. Two further fields were purchased, plus other land and cottages at Wickford, and a greenhouse built with brick and two more cottages.9

The news of the Purleigh colony's success spread, and it was frequently visited by prominent socialists of the time, including George Lansbury. Like the Maryland colony it was admired for its apparent economic success as much as its political idealism. By February 1898 it had grown to include sixty-five members scattered across the surrounding area. There was considerable press interest, including in the *Daily News* and *Manchester Guardian,* with the *Clarion* adopting a predictably critical tone, describing the settlement as having 'jumped the chasm from competition to co-operation without waiting for the plank of social democracy and to have arrived at the shores of anarchism.'10 Yet Purleigh remained admired in some socialist and progressive circles, and was inundated with applications from prospective settlers Its ambitious expansion plans continued with 700 apple trees being planted, 250 gooseberry bushes, a kitchen garden created with celery and potatoes, we all as keeping cows and hens, with more cottages being built.11

A report on the offshoot at Wickford run on similar lines, provided a somewhat optimistic view:

> Every member shall work and cultivate his land on the lines she may think best. Cooperatives will spring up naturally when people of similar aims and ideas get together; the land will be conveyed to each separately, and in fact perfect freedom is the watchword of the colony.12

But in reality there were disagreements among members at both Wickford and Purleigh, and a dissident group led by Samuel Veale Bracher, a young Quaker journalist, broke away in 1898 to start their own colony in the Cotswolds. This became the Whiteway colony near Gloucester, also founded on Tolstoyan principles of common ownership, self-sufficiency, pacifism and vegetarianism.

The estate consisted of about 40 acres, and Bracher purchased the seeds, tools, materials and provisions to get the pioneers started. To begin they all lived communally at Whiteway Hall, while the title deeds to the estate were ceremoniously destroyed as a symbol of the commitment to common ownership. The first settlers were mainly refugees from Purleigh and Wickford, determined to learn from the mistakes made there and overcome problems of communal living. The authority of the state was not recognized, while couples entered into free unions instead of legal marriage. Some buildings were brought in from the outside, such as a large converted army hut transported from Salisbury Plain.

Although originally founded on the principle of gender equality, this did not extend to the domestic tasks of cooking, cleaning and washing clothes. All the women contributed equally to the work in the fields, but also had exclusive responsibility for domestic tasks. One of the original settlers, Nellie Shaw, related how this led to the women rebelling, and was one of the reasons for the increasing individualism among the community. Other disagreements arose over practical decision-making on crop planting and the work schedules, and as a result more changes crept into the lifestyle with small groups building their own wooden cabins, and land being broken up into smaller plots. However, Shaw argued that this was a sensible adaptation to changing circumstances rather than signs of the failure of the original ideals, which the community regarded as remaining largely intact.13

Some of the shacks were converted from chicken and cow sheds, and one building was made entirely from bacon crates bought from Smithfield Market in London, and put together like building blocks. This phase lasted through the First World War, and afterwards new settlers arrived and the community flourished even more in the 1920s. The small wooden cabins were improved and well maintained, the plots were well cultivated as were the gardens attached to each home. A school was built in 1920 where the children were taught according to progressive educational principles, but this project was short-lived due to lack of funding although the community educated their own children until 1936. Despite the increasing individualism among some members which caused tensions, much of the activity at Whiteway remained communal. In 1925 Conway Hall was constructed as the center of cultural and social activity, which continued for many years.14

There were perhaps inevitably some rumours locally about the behavior of the community, and these came to the attention of the police and the Home Office, which bizarrely came to see it as a security risk. The local police were probably more concerned with the prurient gossip about nude sun-bathing and lax moral behavior. A local police report of 1925 stated that the colony members had no manners and their behavior was beastly, but no evidence was cited. The police even paid a husband and wife team to infiltrate the community in the hope of finding some evidence of illegal activity, but most local people interviewed seemed to regard the settlers as harmless cranks rather than subversives.15

9   Building a house at Whiteway

Until the end of the 1920s Whiteway was largely an horticultural community, but its base widened when a group joined from Holt in Norfolk and a Handicraft Guild was formed. An old RAF hut was adapted for use as a workshop, and also home working and crafts were developed such as leather goods, weaving, knitting, metal work and furniture-making. The quality of the work was of a high standard, and exhibitions were held in London to some acclaim. There was also a communal bakery, a co-operative gardening group, a youth club, as well as a football team and other social and cultural groups. But the Whiteway colony remained essentially a working horticultural settlement with the bungalows and cabins set amid vegetable plots covering the 40 acres, the men often bearded and dressed in shorts and sandals in the summer, the women in trousers and boots.16

To be successful and consistent in its principles, a truly egalitarian community needed members who were tolerant and considerate at all times to the needs and views of others. They had to be unselfish, and willing to sacrifice personal desires for the greater good of community harmony. This proved quite difficult at times given the vagaries of human nature, and there was a tendency for a drift towards individualism, and a wish by some to throw off the constraints of collective decision-making. Not everyone could be relied upon to do their fair share of communal labour, and disputes arose over the allocation of tasks, for example at harvest times. So, although the colony might continue, it underwent subtle changes of emphasis, and in a rather different form than the original founders intended.

There were also occasional disagreements over the differing objectives of a community, sometimes between the founder(s) and the other members. This occurred at the Starnthwaite Mills socialist colony set up in 1892 by the Rev. Herbert V. Mills, a Unitarian minister who wanted to try to implement a socialist experiment in communal living. It was quite a large undertaking involving community living, work at the Starnthwaite Mill itself, and on a 127 acre farm nearby. But there was a conflict between the more idealistic socialists in the community and the Rev Mills, who wanted to give more priority to providing the unemployed with useful work to keep them off poor relief. The colony did not survive for long, and in 1891 it was disbanded.[17]

It had recently been argued that the large number of utopian communities set up in the late nineteenth centuries were a response to what appeared to be a pivotal moment, when capitalism stood on the cusp of radical change that was becoming irreversible. The massive growth in urbanization, factory production, mechanization and materialism had brought a permanent end to the old ways of life, but had failed to provide for the spiritual well-being of the people, or even delivered prosperity for all. The reaction was to set up colonies that were an attempt to reconstruct life along communal lines, reviving older ways of farming, market gardening, horticulture and manufacturing, with a rejection of modern life and values.[18]

This was exemplified at the Clousden Free Community and Cooperative colony set up near Newcastle in 1895. The settlers here were influenced by the socialist idealism of Morris together with the anarchism of Peter Kropotkin. They grew peas, cauliflowers, celery, cabbages, and carrots on four acres, planted fruit trees, and grew strawberries on a quarter of an acre. They also cultivated flowers, growing chrysanthemums, roses and even orchids in greenhouses they built themselves. This required long hours of work, up to nineteen hours a day at times, and although the amount of work each individual did was voluntary, most of the settlers joined in. But here too disagreements over political issues led in 1898 to the break-up of the community.[19]

During the First World War many pacifist and conscientious objectors, some of whom were also socialists, sought refuge in communities where they could live and practice their beliefs in rural surroundings. After the introduction of conscription in 1916, they were socially ostracized, and the less fortunate were imprisoned. Others sought refuge far from the crowded town and cities, safe from the prying eyes of officials or crowds of troublemakers accusing them of cowardice or worse. Working on the land was seen as an acceptable alternative to fighting in the war, by pacifists at least, nurturing and growing rather than taking part in the capitalist war-machine.

With the coming of peace, some pacifists who had experience of working on farms wanted to continue working the land in a cooperative endeavor. They believed that communal behavior would counter the selfish individualism of capitalism. Some like Max Plowman, an officer who had survived the conflict, were convinced that a return to the land offered a hope of future survival and avoidance of war. Another idealist with similar views was the writer and critic John Middleton Murry, who had been in a relationship with the writer Katherine Mansfield. The couple had tried communal living of a simple rustic kind in a cottage they shared with D.H. Lawrence and Frieda at Higher Tregerthen near Zennor in Cornwall. But there were personal tensions, and the experiment failed leading to their departure.

Murry became the editor of the *Athenaeum* in 1919, and founded another literary magazine, *Adelphi,* in 1923. By 1929 it was being edited by Richard Rees and the literary editor was Max Plowman. They published new writers including George Orwell and working-class writers such as Jack Common. The magazine was associated with the Left, and the editorial stance invariably reflected the views of

Murry about socialism and communitarianism. Although the readers of *Adelphi* or Murry's other magazine, *Peace News,* were by no means all socialist, they were generally idealists who placed cooperation and community above competition.

In 1935 Murry decided to put his ideals into practice by purchasing a farm at Langham in Essex, and making Max Plowman the manager. It was known as the 'Adelphi Centre', and intended to be a training base for community socialism:

> It can be accomplished only by actual cooperation in actual ordinary human work. No such socialist centre can be rally living until each member, or guest, takes as an obvious duty his full share, according to his capacity, of the actual work of the place; nor can it be truly healthy until it becomes largely self-supporting in the simple necessities of life.20

In its brief existence as a socialist experiment in communal living, the Adelphi Centre suffered from an inherent conflict between the need for practical organization and the ideals of its founder and manager. Plowman was a cerebral idealist with less interest in, or experience of, the details of running a self-sufficient farming community. It was disbanded in 1937 as Murry's interest in the peace movement increased, and he made the property available to the Peace Pledge Union to use as accommodation for refugee Basque children from the Spanish civil war. Later, during the Second World War, it accommodated conscientious objectors in very basic conditions.21

John Middleton Murry continued to believe in the principles of co-operative living however, perhaps partly because he was so detached from the practical problems of making such a community work. He personally never lived on the settlement, preferring to stay more comfortably at a Norfolk vicarage. He believed that eliminating wasteful competition, and replacing it with co-operation, would lead to social progress and the reduction of conflict. The search for profit would be replaced by self-sufficient production to ensure full-employment and release people from long hours of labour. And yet he still thought a strong leader-figure was needed to take command in this new society, to formulate objectives and allocate tasks. They needed to be natural leaders, equipped with imagination and sensitive to the needs of others, commanding respect who would be followed. If all came together successfully, the community could 'transform the

the individualistic and anti-social pseudo-religion of acquisitive society by the grueling and genuinely religious experience of the demands of fraternity.'22

This had echoes of Robert Blatchford, William Morris and several others who looked for self-sufficient communalism to transform the individual and the ills of capitalist society. The transformative impact of pure socialism was the end-result, creating a higher spiritual level of human consciousness where art and culture was able to permeate all aspects of people's lives. People would work to survive, or from choice, rather than over-producing to provide surplus profits for the owners of capital, and would then be free to enrich their lives in whichever way they chose.

Murry carried on with his experiment in co-operative living at Langham in the 1930's,increasingly emphasizing its role as a pacifist haven as the threat of war from Europe grew. The emphasis on socialism may have been diluted somewhat, but the old idealism remained intact. The thirty members of the colony lived in dormitories, ate their meals and worked in the fields together, undertaking a fair share of all the tasks involved. There were now quite a range of people including Quakers, Plymouth Brethren, Catholic vegetarians, and cycling enthusiasts. This wide range of personal beliefs and interests was held together by a common belief in pacifism, but there was no consensus by then about socialism.23

When this arrangement eventually proved unsustainable, Murry established yet another colony, this time at Thaxted in Norfolk. It was 1942 when he purchased Lodge Farm, and began writing about the travails of setting it up in *Community Farm*. As in his previous efforts Murry adopted a rather Olympian detachment from the detailed daily problems of running the place, and seemed more interested in railing against the iniquities of capitalism, with its factory work, dehumanizing mechanization and unemployment. The others, however, found it difficult to reconcile the high principles behind the project at Thaxted with the hard work of digging trenches and being up to the ankles in mud. There were some committed socialists, but it was largely a pacifist community and the old tensions arose among people of different political persuasions. There was also a personal animosity towards Murry, resentment about their dependence on him as the main provider and as the mainly absentee property-owner.24

Apart from the land colonies there was also a desire among some working-class people in the cities to build their own place in the countryside. These people were not self-consciously socialist, but their need to reconnect with rural roots and escape the confines of city life had a similar inspiration as the early socialist land colonists. They were not motivated by ideals of communal living, and tended to be rugged individualists seeking their own private utopia. Before 1914 there were examples of un-regulated land squatting by migrants from the cities, but after 1918 these accelerated in remote areas along river estuaries, by lakes and on the sandy shorelines of the coast.

The 1918 promise of 'homes fit for heroes' made by Lloyd George did not become a reality for most, and there was little official support for improved housing or employment. A newspaper report in 1922 quoted an ex-soldier, living with his wife and four children under canvas with makeshift facilities, as saying, 'If they told me in France that I should come back to this I wouldn't have believed it.'25 The bitterness was palpable, and the lack of policies or hope offered by the post-war government saw a surge in support for Labour, and a decision by some to take matters into their own hands.

These plotland housing settlements were unplanned and uncoordinated, but were eventually found all over the country creating a landscape of low-density shacks, bungalows and other structures. The builders sometimes used surplus army materials, such as huts and bell-tents left over from the war, or old train carriages painted and converted to house a whole family. By the mid-1930s settlements could be seen across the North Downs and along the Thames estuary, with many East Londoners settling in place such as Pitsea, Lainden, Rayleigh, Jaywick Sands and Canvey island. There were also settlements along the south coast from Exmouth to Shoreham, at Peacehaven and Camber Sand, as well as inland in parts of Sussex and Kent. Mancunians made for the fringes of the Pennines at Marple and Mottram, and there were settlements along the Severn Valley and in Lakeland settings.26

The appeal of these settlements was on one level to enjoy rural or coastal seclusion well away from slum housing and squalid urban conditions, but they can also be seen as a revolt against the poverty of urban working class life between the wars. They were less concerned about the ownership of land as an end in itself, and more with creating a small ideal world of the settlers own choosing.27 They remained poor, and conditions were invariably primitive with often no running water, gas, electricity or main sewer connections. The cooking and heating was usually by paraffin stove, and in winter the cold and damp added to the discomforts. But they were now independent and free of the landlordism under which they had struggled in the slums, and from which they sought to escaped.

These unregulated 'eyesores' alarmed outsiders, were scorned by aesthetes, and perceived as a threat by the largely middle and upper-class army of preservationists and conservationists. Their organizations were burgeoning in the 1930s, such as The National Trust, the Council for the Preservation of Rural England, and the Men of the Trees, while country landowners were aghast at their proliferation and lobbied against them. Some of the criticism was little more than a patronizing protest at the social behavior of working-class people who had the temerity to colonize what had previously been isolated and deserted wild places. Some of the criticism came from unexpected quarters, such as Cyril Joad, was scathing about the litter, open air cooking and eating, as well as the noise made by the working-classes at leisure in the country including their propensity to undress given the opportunity. The messages was that access was fine but it should be organized, tutored, and never random and ucontrolled.28

George Lansbury, coming to the East End from rural Essex as a child, sympathized with the desire of Londoners who wanted to re-connect with the countryside. As the reforming socialist Mayor of Poplar doing his best to protect local people from unemployment, homelessness, and poverty he developed close connections with the community at Jaywick Sands. He took an interest in these communities, and in the efforts of East Enders to improve their lives in this way on the abandoned farmlands coastal borderlands of south Essex. Lansbury had absorbed the rural nostalgia of the labour movement, and believed in the reviving effects of contact with nature. Soon after becoming leader of the Labour Party in1934 he wrote that he longed 'to see a start made on the job of reclaiming, recreating rural England.'29

The early socialists did not seek to monopolize the land, or deprive others of it, but sought to have it redistributed more equally as they believed the resources of nature should be fairly available for all. Not only were large land holdings ethically untenable, largely based on wrongful misappropriation, (i.e. theft) in the past, but also economically inefficient. Such a finite resource need protecting by the state, to prevent the ravages of the free-market depriving the vast majority of the people of their birthright. Some form of land nationalization remained Labour Party policy for most of the twentieth century, but until it could be implemented, many socialists sought their own solutions living communally and putting down roots in the countryside. This was a strong impulse for some, including non-socialists, who shared with them the desire to be free from landlordism, and to create their own small arcadias in rural surroundings.

5. GARDEN CITIES AND ALLOTMENTS

Another form of human settlement infused with socialist idealism was the garden city movement. The man who was its inspiration, Ebenezer Howard, was a Fabian socialist who had inherited many of the assumptions about the efficacy of the countryside on people resettled from the city. To Howard part of the solution to the appalling urban housing conditions of the nineteenth century was to create new urban communities in the countryside, improving living conditions and re-connecting people with a rural environment. This process would, he hoped, transform their spiritual as well as their physical conditions. This social imperative underlay all his work for he was as much a social reformer as an urban planner, and had inherited the socialist idealism of his predecessors. He had been influenced by Henry George's ideas expressed in his *Progress and Poverty,* that the land properly belonged to the community, and a centralized government organization was needed to ensure this vital resource was reallocated for the benefit of these communities.[1]

Howard had been instrumental in setting up the Garden Cities Association in 1899, and there were several socialists at the inaugural meeting. These included Alexander Payne and Alfred Bishop of the Land Nationalization Society, while also present was J. Bruce Wallace founder of the cooperative Brotherhood Church. The GCA set about campaigning for the building of homes that were healthy and beautiful in communities containing the best of the countryside and the town. These new towns in the countryside would exist for the benefit of their inhabitants rather than commerce and industry, and they would enjoy 'all the beauties and delights of the country.[2]Howard envisaged the purchase of 6000 acres of farmland and the building of houses with gardens on about a thousand of these acres. The rest would encircle the homes with protected and productive farmland turned into working farm units. The housing was to be sympathetically designed to mold into the rural surroundings, rustic in style with the importance of the gardens and landscaping emphasized.[2]

They were to be in effect new colonies of city folk transplanted into the countryside, along lines recommended by Morris and Ruskin. The Morris ideal of people living in 'little communities among green fields, so you can be in the country in a five minute walk' was an evident influence.₃This sentiment was still being echoed in the 1930s by socialists in and outside the Labour Party, and was a constant recurring theme. Hugh Dalton wrote in 1933 that he wanted 'a Merrie England in which every Englishman will live within reasonable distance of green fields instead of within the heart of the slums.'₄

The aim was also philanthropic to provide regular employment at higher wages in healthier surroundings. It was hoped the idyllic environment would attract the 'right' kind of employers: ethical manufacturers, cooperative societies, engineers, architects and many other occupations and professions. The prosperity thus generated would increase the purchasing power of the inhabitants and create demand for the products of the surrounding farms, a large market that was nearby. The ideal was a healthier and natural lifestyle generated by a special combination of country and town and on land that was owned by the local municipal authority.

In Howard's book, *Tomorrow: A Peaceful Path to Real Reform,* social and urban reform were closely linked. The importance of fresh air, and natural beauty to complement well-designed houses and amenities, was essential if the objective of a better society was to be achieved. The town and the country were to be integrated into an organic whole so that the beginning of one and the start of another was a seamless progress, and the rural/urban divide broken down as far as possible. The size of the new towns would be limited, and uncontrolled suburban expansion made impossible by strict zoning regulations of green farming belts. This was necessary to combine the best of the town with the best that the country had to offer. The land was owned by the trustees and the houses leased to the residents with, it was hoped, a proper sense of ownership and community involvement.₅

Howard illustrated his ideas with the 'three magnets' diagram representing the 'country', the 'town' and the country-town'. The attractions of the town include closer proximity to employment, higher wages, as well as amusements, but are off-set by a closing off of nature, human isolation, high rents and prices, long hours of work, unemployment, polluted air, and slum dwellings. The country has many virtues including the beauty of the natural world, fresh air, low rents, and an abundance of natural resources like water. But here is also a lack of human contact, under use of land, restrictions of access like trespass laws, lack of sanitation, no amusements and deserted villages. The town-country magnet however, can combine the best of both while eliminating the disadvantages. There can be provision for the beauty of nature, opportunities for socializing, fields and parks, low rates and prices, pure air and drinking water, a steady flow of capital, bright clean homes for all, public health facilities, freedom

10 Ebenezer Howard, The Three Magnets No 1 1902
Garden Cities of Tomorrow

and co-operation. It is clear that Howard was a theorist with a social purpose, and that his plans for garden cities were based on a strong critique of unfettered free-market capitalism, not least for overlooking the needs of the people. If the whole of society could be re-organized around a network of garden cities, the grip of capitalism would be loosened, and a more cooperative socialist alternative arise out the preferences and needs of the people.6

But he thought the lead still needed to be taken by enlightened reformers like himself, and planning was the key to ensure developments adopted the core requirement of a belt of farm land around the city. By 1903Howard and Henry Harvey Vivian, his partner in the co-partnership housing movement, had attracted enough public support and funding to begin the building of Letchworth. The Garden Cities Association ran a campaign for the collection of funds, and many contributors were socialists and liberal reformers attracted to this planned solution to the problems of urban slum housing. A company was formed called 'The First Garden City Ltd' which purchased 3826 acres in Hertfordshire for £160,378, and later more land purchased to increase this to 4710 acres. This was still rather less than Howard had originally recommended, but it was a very spacious design, even though the architecture was criticized as being uninspiring and uniform.7

Howard wanted Letchworth to be the model for the future. and hoped it would inspire the construction of many other examples of garden cities. He wanted to promote harmony and community through localism, and social control by the people themselves, a kind of social vision without state involvement. Another aim was to regenerate the depressed and de-populated countryside as well as liberate the congested urban slum dwellers, and from 'a joyous union of town and country would come soaring new hope, a new civilization'.8

The designs of the architect, Raymond Unwin, harked back to the rural past of previous times, a vision of the medieval village of pre-industrial times. This conception of the village community represented to Howard and Unwin cooperative harmony and balance, expressing more of a communal than individualistic way of life. The architectural theme was rustic, and even the windows and interiors were meant to evoke a medieval cottage style. Although housing density was kept low at twelve homes an acre, a communal vision only extended to the working-class cottages to rent, while the middle-class housing was physically separated from them. There was a need to attract professional and skilled people in sufficient numbers, and in respect pragmatism was given precedence over socialist idealism.

Howard was less directly involved in Welwyn, built in 1920, about twenty miles from London, but it was also planned on similar lines to emphasize the charm of the countryside with easy access, and plenty of green open space. The architecture was also partly rustic, with pleasant cottages reminiscent of the arts and craft movement. It had wide roads together with the zoning of residential, business and industrial areas. For Howard's ideas to work in practice there was a need of social investment, which at the time government would not provide, and private investment insisted on a commercial return. It was in fact marketed as a middle-class town convenient for commuters to London, while two key criteria for the success of a garden city were missing: the town was never self-sufficient, and never enjoyed the mix of social classes.8

Apart from Howard's two garden cities, another project inspired by some of his ideas was Hampstead Garden suburb built on243 acres in North London from 1906. It was inspired by Samuel and Henrietta Barnett who also employed Raymond Unwin to design it, and was originally intended to be for all social classes and incomes. The houses, which were larger and better appointed than at Letchworth, were to be separated only by hedges and there was to be plenty of woods and public gardens open to all. But the area was already a London suburb, and no effort was made to make it self-sufficient. In any case, property values ensured that the area soon became the preserve of the well-off middle-class, and any lingering idealism was soon obliterated by the property market. The main residual influence of Howard was on the planning community, and on the new towns built in the twenty-five years after 1945. The basic egalitarian socialism, and concern for the effect of country living upon working-class urban dwellers was still found in these projects, even if nowhere near on the scale envisaged by Howard.9

The influence of Howard's socialist utopianism and the garden village movement found an echo in the communities built by enlightened employers for their workers. These employers were certainly not socialists but they shared the same views about the need for creating ideal environments for people. They thought that clean well-designed housing and a sense of community was desirable in itself, but would also result in more contented and productive workers. Following in the footsteps of William Lever and George Cadbury was Francis Crittall, a manufacturer of the metal-framed windows so ubiquitous in 1930's housing, who created a model village for his workers at Silver End in Essex from 1926 to 1932. The houses contained some advanced examples of European modernism, painted white with flat roofs and with Crittall metal windows. They were well designed and provided modern amenities, well in advance of other working class housing of the time. There was also an attempt to instill a sense of community and village life. A commemorative oak was planted by the Labour Prime Minister Ramsay MacDonald, and there was a thatched tea shop and tennis courts. The aim was an 'ideal' environment combining the ideals of Howard with Thomas Lever's Port Sunlight and Cadbury's Bourneville. Thomas Bata, the Czech shoe magnate, did something similar in East Tilbury in the 1930s where he built a large new shoe factory and housed his worker's in well-designed modern housing influenced by Bauhaus design. But these were also paternalistic experiments by enlightened employers who needed to house their workers close to their new factories where no previous housing existed. They were essentially company communities without the utopian zeal of Robert Owen, and while the workers may have appreciated their new homes, the motives of Crittall and Bata, like Lever and the Cadbury's at Bourneville, were infused with enlightened self-interest.[10]

The housing conditions of agricultural workers was always of a very poor standard, with low levels of hygiene and overcrowding common. There was also the problem of insecurity and lack of independence due to the tied tenancy system, which provided no real security. Thatched country cottages were romanticized at the time but they were often damp and inconvenient, lacking basic amenities. There was though an inclination for socialists and progressives to include rustic cottages in their idealized picture of country life, as the designs for the housing in Letchworth reveal. There were a few good houses for retired farm workers, such as the cottages built in Dorset by the TUC in 1934 to commemorate the centenary of the Tolpuddle Martyrs, which were praised for their design and comfort. But these were the exception, and much of Labour Party's appeal to the agricultural vote in the 1920s and 30s included the promise to improved village and farm housing.[11]

The first Labour government passed the Housing Act of 1924, that attempted to do something about country slums through higher grants for agricultural housing. The act also required county councils to make contributions to district councils for the building of rural housing. The 1929 Labour government also planned an increase in new house building in the countryside by 40,000, but very few were completed before the plan were cancelled by National Government in 1931.Poor and inadequate housing was one aspect of the inequality between town and country, and prevented any hope that existed on the Left of closing this gap and ending the tied cottage system.

The vast majority of the urban working-class were unable to enjoy the countryside, and there only contact with nature had to come from within their immediate area. One solution was to rent an allotment, and the number had increased considerably since 1880. They had originally been provided by landowners so their tenants could grow food, and they would not be a burden of the parish. But some farmers claimed they were a distraction for their workers, and sometimes accused them of stealing seeds and tools.[8]Whenthe franchise was extended to agricultural workers in 1884, courting their votes became more important, and providing allotments was one means of persuasion used by candidates for election to county councils

Although initially a rural phenomenon, allotments became more common in the suburbs and in the inner city areas. The urban working-class may have been cut off from the countryside, but the country could be brought into the city, even if it was only a small amount of land under intensive cultivation. The municipal councils used new powers under the 1908 Small Holdings and Allotments Act to provide allotments spaces, and the number grew to 600,000 by 1913. During the First World War their number reached 1.5 million, and in Second World War 1.75 million, with official government support to increase food production. That allotments had become an important source of supplementary food for the table was made clear in Seebohm Rowntree's survey of agricultural labourers in the Midlands in 1913, and which revealed the paucity of their diet. Without allotments some of the poor would have starved, but in any case the health of the working class was generally appalling as the medical examination of military recruits in 1914 revealed.12

As urban allotments became more popular, the provision was increasingly politicized, and a spate of local government laws after 1880 extended the obligation of local authorities to provide more of them. This fit well with the municipal socialism of the time, and ensured that Labour-controlled councils such as Poplar and West Ham in east London made full use of their powers, while 25% of all authorities provided land for allotments.13 In Poplar the council actively encouraged local allotment and horticultural production. The local councilors were involved, and the Mayor presented the prizes at horticultural shows such as the Millwall and Cubitts Town Horticultural Society show, while the local paper reported that he and the judges 'expressed genuine approval of the quality of the cauliflowers, onions, cabbages, carrots, beans and beetroot.'14

The state took a more interventionist role in the economy and society during the First World War, and there was an even more concerted effort to ensure more allotments were producing food. In the wake of the Cultivation of Lands Act of 1915, a new wave of allotments swept the country. Model plots were set up to encourage this process, even in Kensington Gardens, and railway land was re-claimed for cultivation. By 1919, the number of new applications for plots was running at 7,000 a week.15 In 1917, the socialist councilors of Poplar were doing all they could to protect the interests of the plot holders by keeping rents low, and continuing to keep close links with them. They were also prepared to represent the plot holders in their relations private or non-council landlords as, for example, in May 1918 on a fencing issue on land in Millwall owned by the Port of London Authority. 16

The Poplar Borough Council encouraged new allotment growth in particular in the area between Bromley-by-Bow and Stratford, so much so that it became known locally as 'Allotment Town.' On Sundays the whole community would go down to their allotment sheds which were little 'home from homes' with carpeting, chairs and glazed, and tea-making facilities.17 Again, the council did all it could to ensure the scheme prospered, and a considerable camaraderie developed between the councilors and plot holders. In 1935, George

Lansbury, local MP and former Mayor, was so popular that he received 80% of the votes cast in the general election. All the local councilors, and the two MP's for the area, were from the same working class background as the allotment holders. Their occupations included 'stevedores, housewives, toolmakers, labourers, corn porters, railwaymen, postmen, and engineers.' This narrowed the gap between councilors and local residents and helped to create more class solidarity.[18]

19   Cultivating an Urban Allotment in the 1930s

There was also a good deal of co-operation between the plot holders and the local allotment associations which encouraged another level of local democracy, with elected committees and devolved decision-making. This co-operation extended to sharing plants and sharing out surplus produce among members. There were local and district competitions for flowers, vegetables and fruit which also tended to increase a sense of outdoor communalism. In 1921 this social class solidarity led to the rates rebellion in Poplar in which six councilors went to prison for refusing to set what they saw as an unfairly high rate.[18]

During the inter-war years local allotments, continued to make a real difference to living standards of poor local communities, both

11 William Morris

12 Robert Blatchford

13 Walter Crane

14 Cecil Sharp

Margaret McMillan

15 Margaret McMillan   16   Ebenezer Howard

17 Cyril Joad   18 John Fletcher Dodd

rural and urban, particularly areas of rising unemployment. In 1928 there were 300,000 unemployed miners alone, mostly in South Wales, with re-employment impossible in mining villages dependent on the pits. They and their families were facing starvation, and allotments were seen as a way of providing the families with food. This appalling situation led the Quaker Society of Friends to set up a Coalfields Distress Committee, helping unemployed men with starting the cultivation of allotments. There were soon 203 allotment societies in the South Wales area, and by 1929 1,600 tons of potato seeds were being distributed to allotment holders, along with tons of beans, peas and seeds of all kinds. The scheme spread elsewhere, and by 1930 there were 15,000 allotment holders in Sheffield who could rent their plots for 2d per week with nothing to pay for six months. Some of the plots were highly productive in food, but also with flowers which could be sold.[19]

The decision was taken to expand the scheme after a meeting in London at which Ramsay MacDonald, and Christopher Addison, the Minister of Agriculture, made speeches. Addison was so impressed with the scheme that he incorporated it into the Agricultural Land (Utilisation) Act of 1931 as a temporary measure. Now that government was involved the Quaker Allotments Committee became the National Allotments Committee. To the government the scheme was seen as a way of providing food and keeping the unemployed occupied, also an inexpensive way of being seen to do something, as well as countering the influence of the Communist Party, still strong in some mining areas. But after a year the government withdrew, leaving the Society of Friends to carry on with the work alone. By 1935 the 'Allotment Gardens for the Unemployed Scheme' covered most of the country, and over 120,000 men were helped, growing produce worth an estimated £600,000.[20]

Allotments remained popular with the working class all over the country throughout the 1930s, and from 1939 they were once again given impetus by the needs of the Home Front. A 'Dig for Victory' campaign was launched by the government to increase self-sufficiency and expand food production. The aim was to increase new allotments and to use pasture land, railway land, parkland, and gardens, disused air fields and sports grounds, including Lords cricket ground which was dug up. There was an enthusiastic response by people in town and country, encouraged by Ministry of Information films and pamphlets. These not only encouraged food cultivation, but demonstrated how vegetables could be used in all kinds of cookery, and as a substitute for meat which was in short supply. This renewed interest and activity in reconnecting people with the soil was an echo of the past, but this time the sponsor was the government and not idealistic individuals. The effectiveness of state power in mobilizing human and physical resources for the war effort impressed the planners, and emboldened the Labour Party in drafting its 1945 manifesto.21

Apart from allotments, gardens and gardening were thought by early socialists to be inherently beneficial for people, and exposure to flowers, shrubs, trees and the natural world a necessary counterweight to their daily working lives. The provision of public parks was part of the 'municipal socialism' of Joseph Chamberlain in Birmingham together with other civic improvements such as slum clearance, clean water supply and sewage disposal. Municipal swimming pools and parks laid out with lower beds, boating lakes and bandstands was considered as important as the new museums, art galleries and public libraries

Most of the urban working class could not access an allotment even if they wished to do so, there was always a shortage of plots and there was also the rental cost. Although they were found in all urban areas, even those of maximum deprivation and poverty such as Bethnal Green and Bow in east London, the supply was never sufficient to meet the demand. The long hours of work and consequent lack of leisure time made cultivating a plot difficult for some, and tending a garden was not always possible. Most working-class terraced housing only had a back-yard, invariably concreted over which provided space for the family bath to be stored and for the outdoor lavatory block. There was rarely enough space to lay out and cultivate a garden, and the new blocks of council flats may only have had a small balcony on which a few plants could be cultivated in pots. However the London County Council did what it could to encourage its working-class tenants to take an interest in gardening through the 'London Gardens Society' by organizing competitions for the best kept gardens, and in 1938 about 650,000 people entered the 'All Garden Championships'.

The LCC architects department did its best to include gardens for new council houses, but most of the large new developments of the 1930's consisted of large blocks of council flats. Even so, the LCC architects tried to find space for the tenants to cultivate a communal garden and these were invariably well-kept with colourful displays of flowers throughout the summer. If this was not possible, then some kind of landscaping was included within the development.22

The desire to get the people back to the land and nature, inherited form the eighteenth century and earlier, was reflected in the projects of early socialist planners and architects. Their ideal socialist society was a rural or semi-rural one, self-sufficient and craft-based, and free from the corrupting influence of industrial capitalism and the big cities. It was encouraged by the sense of the people being robbed of the right to own and access to their own country, and the need to redress these injustices. The garden city movement, and progressive planning in the LCC, for example, incorporated some of these ideals which were continued in the new towns built after 1945. But it was also present in the provision and encouragement of allotments whether in country, suburb or town, that offered the chance of partial self-sufficiency. The allotment also gave the opportunity of getting back on the land, albeit in an urban context and on limited space, helped to supplement the family food supply and encouraged co-operation and a sense of community.

6. SUMMER SCHOOLS AND COUNTRY HOUSES

The idea of providing an educational experience in a rural holiday atmosphere originated in the United States in the nineteenth century. These 'summer schools' as they were termed were usually held on college campuses during the long summer vacation, when most of the students and staff were absent. Although often academic in content the courses also offered various outdoor activities in addition, such as trekking, canoeing and climbing. The first summer schools in Britain were arranged in 1888 by the University Extension movement based in Oxford, with the aim of reaching students from a wider catchment area and social class. The idea was adopted by other organizations such as the Workers Educational Association, but it was the Fabian Society that started the first political summer schools.1

The Fabians were influenced by the German Social Democrats who held ambitious educational programmes as early as 1891. These involved lecture courses held in scenic locations supplemented with concerts, dramatic productions, and walks in the mountains. Despite this influence, summer schools in Britain developed a 'peculiarly Anglo-Saxon combination of holiday, sociability and more or less intellectual effort'2 The Fabian summer schools began in 1907, partly through pressure by H.G. Wells, to encourage the participation of younger members carrying on the struggle for socialism in the next generation. It led to the creation of the 'Nursery' by Rosamund Brand as an educational branch for young Fabians under twenty-eight. The Nursery hired halls for meetings and organized lecture courses on subjects to do with the meaning and practice of socialism, although the executive was always kept informed about the content.

The Fabian Summer schools, however, enjoyed a semi-autonomous status and in the early years were organized by a committee of six chaired by Dr. F. Lawson Dodds. They raised the finance to purchase a large country house in North Wales which could serve as the base for summer schools. For five years leading up to 1918 schools were

held every August and September, with others at Easter lasting up to
a week or two. Apart from the lectures, various other outdoor
activities were arranged, many of them involved healthy doses of
fresh air such as hiking, climbing, and swimming. Several thousand
young people attended Fabian summer schools before 1918, and they
proved highly popular.3

In 1911 the Fabians held a summer school in the more bracing air
of Switzerland where the holiday spirit appears to have prevailed over
too much serious study. The alpine surroundings provided plenty of
opportunity for more strenuous mountain climbing and walking. The
country had been popular since the nineteenth century with the new
middle-class tourists, and also with reading parties and study groups
organized by individual dons at Oxford and Cambridge colleges.
These involved groups of half a dozen or so undergraduates staying
in mountain huts on the lower slopes, and doing all the cooking and
domestic tasks. The idea was to combine a self-catering holiday with
the scenic beauty providing an inspiration for reading and study. This
may have influenced the Fabians to choose the location for the 1911
summer school, but the experiment was not repeated with the First
World War imminent.4

The Fabian summer schools proved so popular they were
continued throughout the war years, and in 1917 a new guest house
was opened in the Lake District. This was a popular location for
outdoor activities in progressive circles, its romantic associations with
Ruskin and Wordsworth adding to the appeal of the glorious scenery,
and it had already been used by the Fabians in 1915 when they rented
a house. Although the aim of the summer school was serious study,
the locations continued to be chosen for the opportunities provided
for plenty of outdoor recreation. The ostensible aim of the summer
school was 'the study of social science and to afford students,
whether avowed socialists or not, an opportunity for meeting and
social intercourse.'5 Later this was amended to 'bringing together
workers in the various grades of society and social conditions for
social mutual intercourse, and to afford the opportunities for courses
of lectures, debates and conversations dealing with the most modern
problems of sociology and economics. While study is the great object
of the school it is not forgotten that recreation will be needed for
those who come here.'6

By 1919 these recreational activities had been integrated more formally into the summer school programme. They were cultural and physical, including concerts, drama, hiking, tennis, cycling, swimming, cycling and many other outdoor activities. The assumption was that healthy outdoor activity of all kinds would help progressive young minds grapple more effectively with the social and economic problems encountered in the lecture room. A pattern was established that remained more or less unchanged for twenty years or so. The students would arrive on Saturday, and after registering and settling in to their accommodation would be addressed by the course director. Each day there would be three or four lectures in the morning, followed by question and answer sessions. After lunch the afternoons were given over to outdoor activities, and Wednesdays were free of lectures for an all-day organized excursion into countryside, usually involving a good deal of walking and hiking, or a trip to a place of historic or cultural interest. In the evenings after dinner, there would be open debates on current affairs and on Fridays the students and staff would put on a dramatic production, usually in costume, or a musical concert.

The students at the summer schools also included non-members and foreign guests, and sometimes local residents were permitted to attend for a small fee. By the 1920s young students predominated, and the guest lecturers were often experts of some kind, including academics and journalists.[7] A regular lecturer was Cyril Joad, at the time still a reluctant civil servant in the board of Trade. He was a member of the Fabian Society and the ILP, and was getting as much teaching experience as possible to try to get a permanent teaching job. Joad had started teaching on Fabian summer schools as early as 1907 when he attended the school at Barrow House near Keswick in the Lake District. He continued doing so throughout the war and for some years after during his summer holiday.

As summer schools became more popular the Fabians took leases on a number of large houses in the country at Godalming in Surrey, Ilkley in Yorkshire, and Thaxted in Essex, among others. There was usually a problem with the accommodation, especially for the women who were thought to need more bathrooms, and regular crises occurred. There were also problems with the catering and finance, but despite these problems the schools prospered. This was probably due to their specific purpose of providing education with a socialist perspective in idyllic surroundings, with plenty of recreation, exercise and opportunities for socializing.8

20   A Fabian Summer School group in the 1920s

In August 1923 a Fabian summer school was being held at Penlea on the south Devon coast. The weather was fine that year, and so warm that some classes were held outside. The students would take mattresses to lie on the cliff edge, although this was frowned on by the organizers who were suspicious of romantic dalliances. The ubiquitous Cyril Joad was present, and on one occasion went for a walk on Dartmoor with two of the female students. They got lost in the mist and rain, missed the last train back, and had no money for a hotel so had to spend the night under a haystack. In the morning they walked the twenty-eight mile return journey, but got an unsmiling and frosty reception. There was a clear suspicion that the getting 'lost' had been deliberate, although they assured the organizers that it had been perfectly innocent, that they were genuinely lost.9

Later that summer, Joad joined a small unofficial Fabian summer at Ravenscar in Yorkshire, where G.D.H. Cole was also lecturing on the prospects for a new Labour government. One afternoon he went for a bracing walk with an elderly organizer and his young female secretary along a coastal path towards Robin Hood Bay. But Joad wanted to turn inland and go over the moors, while the girl agreed to accompany him much to the annoyance of her elder employer. It seems that some of the younger girls at the school responded to the attentions the young lecturer paid to them, and this was not apparently unusual as there was a good deal of socializing between the student and younger lecturers. Some of the young women may have welcomed the opportunity of spending a few weeks away from their families un-chaperoned, and able to mix freely.

However, the gossip eventually reached the ears of Fabian officials in London where there were a few complaints. At Fabian headquarters off Whitehall, Joad came to be regarded as something of a nuisance, despite his popularity as a lecturer and leader of outdoor hikes and treks. His main antagonist was Miss Hankinson, head of the summer school programme, who was concerned about protecting the young female students from being seduced when they should have been absorbing the principles of Fabian socialism. She was not prepared to stand any nonsense, and Joad was warned as to his future conduct.[10]

The young man was called to appear before the summer school committee where he put up a strong defence, admitting to innocent liaisons but playing down anything more serious. But the committee decided to issue him with a formal notice that his attendance would no longer be welcomed. Cyril was extremely upset, not least because he felt he had contributed to the success of the summer schools, and considered a lot of fuss was being made about very little, and that Miss Hankinson was behaving like a Victorian maiden aunt when the Fabian Society should have been in revolt against the old morality.[11]

The average age of summer school students was quite low by the 1920s and there was now competition from the Workers Educational Association, Birkbeck College Adult Educational Department and the ILP, which all organized summer schools. The ILP started its summer schools in 1917, first in collaboration with the Fabians, but then developing their own weekend study groups. These were usually residential and held throughout the year, usually in a rural setting and always combining educational and recreational activities. They had the advantage of being considerably less expensive than longer courses, the first being held in March 1926 when 50 people attended. The programme included lectures, open discussions and country walks in the afternoons. When the group reached a village they would try to hold open socialist propaganda meetings in the evening.11 Although the programme varied, the ILP shared with the Fabians plenty of outdoor activity, with walking, rambling and cycling a feature. In 1924 there were thirty-seven weekend schools held, but a rapid decline set in with the fall in ILP membership at the end of the decade.12

The Labour Party itself did not hold summer schools, but two connected organizations did: the Women's Labour League and the Labour League of Youth. The former was started in 1904 as a semi-independent body but became the women's section of the Labour Party in 1918. Its educational work had begun before then, but was confined initially to local branches with lectures and discussions. In 1924 it held it first summer school, organized along familiar lines with lectures in the morning followed by discussions and afternoons devoted to outdoor recreational activities with the evening given over to music, songs and reading.

The Labour League of Youth began in 1922, and by 1924 was an integral part of the party, effectively its youth wing. It had many branches in the constituencies, and was particularly strong in the London area. The LLY was soon holding weekend schools and summer camps, several a year which were highly popular perhaps because the educational element was regarded as less important than the communal outdoor activities. Apart from providing political education for future leaders, the camps were planned to engender a sense of unity and togetherness, as well as simply providing an enjoyable time. They were spent under canvas in the countryside with trekking and sport, as well as the usual community singing around the camp fire. They were similar to the summer camps held by the youth wings of several European socials democratic parties at the time, including the Norwegian and Swedish.13

The political education provided at these camps was intended to train young socialist politicians for local and national elected power, which after 1931 looked an extremely uncertain. The Labour Party lost heavily in the 1931 general election, and its small rump of MPs were in opposition facing the rows of the National Coalition government members. There was an air of betrayal and disillusion on the mainstream Left, but if power seemed a long off there was still plenty of activity in the youth wing. The Labour League of Youth formed clubs for football, cricket and ladies skittles, cycling and rambling flourished, especially in the North of England where there was a more co-operative tradition in these activities and nearly every weekend was occupied. The future Labour MP and Speaker of the House of Commons, Betty Boothroyd, was a member of the LLY as a young girl in the early 1950s, and later referred to the rambles on Howarth Moor as 'politics and fresh air.'14

The strong connection between outdoor social activities and political education continued throughout the history of the League of Youth, particularly through hill walking over the moors and in the Lake District. In the 1930s many working-class young people of all occupations – plumbers, plasterers, bricklayers, mechanics and many others – were often unemployed with time on their hands, and welcomed the opportunity to go on long treks and discuss current affairs on the way. It was still then assumed that future socialist leaders would come mainly from the working class, and that talent and ability could be found among working class young people to provide future leadership.

In 1934 the League's branch members in London contributed to a fund, supplemented with a grant from Stafford Cripps, to purchase an old semi-derelict Georgian manor house called 'The Geddings' in Hertfordshire. After renovations it provided accommodation for about 80 young people with plenty of outdoor space. The *Labour Magazine* reported in August 1934 that 'hundreds of young people from all parts of the country came to Hoddesdon to live socialism.' The hostel was surrounded by ten acres of gardens and grounds, and had its own management committee and resident warden.

Summer schools remained popular on the left through the 1930s until the outbreak of war. During the last summer of peace in 1939 a Co-operative summer school being held on the North Yorkshire coast. Cyril Joad was present as a lecturer, and he and the students were enjoying the swimming, cricket and long walks on the moors. The announcement that Britain was now at war with Nazi Germany, although expected, was a shock and the students dispersed not knowing when they would be able again to attend a summer school in peacetime.15

The early Labour Party and socialist movement was able to benefit from the patronage of some wealthy people, often former Liberals, who had converted to socialism, and who put their wealth and property at the disposal of the movement. Their substantial properties were used for conferences, weekend political gatherings and summer schools. An early benefactor was H.D. Harben, the heir to the Prudential Insurance Company, who had been a Tory parliamentary candidate in 1900 and stood as a Liberal in 1906, but moved leftwards to become a socialist by 1912. Harben had inherited a large country house and estate at Newlands Park in Buckinghamshire. Apart from the house there was park, farms and six cottages where he entertained many of the leading progressive figures of the day. The Pankhurst's were friends, and suffragettes who had recently been released from prison found sanctuary at Newlands until they had recuperated. They were allowed free run of the place, and other guests from the Bucks county set were surprised to come across some rather haggard looking ex-prisoners walking about the grounds in dressing gowns, talking about their penal experiences.16

Another wealthy convert to socialism anxious to place her considerable acres and energy to the cause was Francis Greville, the Countess of Warwick. Once mistress of the Prince of Wales, Daisy Greville lived a luxurious life at Warwick Castle and in London, as well as Easton Lodge, her estate in Essex. After an extravagant social *Clarion* by Robert Blatchford. Taking deep offence Daisy visited him at his editorial offices in London where, after a discussion, Blatchford apparently converted her to socialism. She became a philanthropist, and in 1904 joined the Marxist Social Democratic Federation, donating money to it and campaigning for several progressive causes including free meals for schoolchildren. As a pacifist, Daisy strongly opposed war in 1914 which brought her into contact with pacifist socialists, mainly in the ILP. After the war she joined the Labour Party, and did what she could to help it gain power, while standing as

Labour candidate, unsuccessfully, at the Warwick and Leamington by-election in 1923.

Her country estate at Easton Lodge at Dunmow in Essex was ideally suited for political and social gatherings, and Daisy more or less placed it at the disposal of the Labour Party for summer schools, conferences and weekend gatherings. It was conveniently close to London, and well served by trains from Liverpool Street station. She was friendly with Beatrice Webb, H.G. Wells and other leading Fabians, and Easton Lodge was also placed at their disposal for educational purposes and policy discussions. Daisy's commitment to socialism and public spirit were much admired by Beatrice Webb, although she had some reservations about accepting the hospitality of a privileged aristocrat. Despite admiring the beauty of the surroundings, Webb was rather wary and her doubts were never entirely resolved. But she was curious, and glad enough to accept the invitation and perhaps even a little eager at the prospect:

> …I have not heard whether the parties at Easton Lodge have been a success or not, except the one the Henderson chaperoned, which he enjoyed. Bur I have been so busy with various matter that I have not had time to go round to the Labour Party office and find out what was happening in regard to Easton Lodge. I gather the arrangements are in the hands of one of the staff under the direction of Mr Henderson. You will see from the enclosed circular that the HCC (Half Moon Club) id proposing to go to Easton Lodge for the weekend of July7. What is suggested is that the executive, together with any husbands who are able to attend, should stay for the weekend, asking the members to come down for a picnic in the woods and tea afterwards at Easton Lodge. We should each bring our lunch so there would be the least possible bother over the the arrangements. I hope that HG and your sons will be there. I should imagine that if the day were fine we should have about 200 - perhaps more, as I think there is a great deal of curiosity about Easton Lodge. Would you be inclined to put up any of the executive in case all decided to come, which would make too large party, I think, for Easton Lodge…17

H.G. Wells accepted the offer to live with his family rent free in a cottage on the estate, while Ramsay MacDonald and other Labour leaders, who acquired the taste for the aristocratic lifestyle, were frequent visitors.

A Pathe Newsreel film from 1923 shows Arthur Henderson, soon to be a minister in the 1924 Labour government, leading a party on a visit to Easton Lodge. They are being shown around the gardens by Lady Warwick, inspecting the round pond and her miniature zoo. The visit was intended to assess the suitability of the place as a permanent Labour conference base in the country, and was meant to be kept secret. But Lady Warwick had informed the news media in advance, hence the newsreel cameras, much to the annoyance of her guests. Her offer was ultimately declined following the 1924 general election on the grounds of cost after the expense of fighting the elections campaign.18

There was a further attempt to donate the house and grounds to the Labour movement by Lady Warwick, and she offered it to the Trades Union Congress. Another tour of inspection was made, this time by trade union leaders, and a proposal was discussed to merge Ruskin College with the National Labour College and move the new body into Easton Lodge. But the move was defeated at the TUC Conference of 1926, again on cost grounds, as it was claimed trade unions funds were so depleted after the General Strike. The house continued to be used for socialist groups, however, including the Fabian Society, the ILP, and the Half Moon Club, a socialist group that had held summer schools throughout the summers between the wars. Anthony Greenwood, son of Arthur Greenwood and later a Cabinet minister who joined the Labour Party at 14, remembered attending socialist gatherings at Easton Lodge in the 1920s. He recalled the lively debates mixed with outdoor activities such as walks, tennis and tugs of war. It was at Easton Lodge, also, that Oswald Mosley, then a Labour MP, and John Strachey formulated a plan for stimulating economic demand based on Keynesian theory they hoped Lbaour would adopt.19

In 1930, a series of conferences was held at Easton Lodge by a group of Fabians with the aim of generating a new sense of socialist purpose by formulating a plan of action for the Labour Party when it formed a government. They were bitterly disappointed with the apparent torpor of the Labour government elected in 1929, unable to find any sort of radical answer to the financial crisis and its effects. From these meetings emerged the Society for Socialist Inquiry and Propaganda (SSIP or 'ZIP') seeking new ways to prepare for a 'real' socialist future Labour government. The members met amid the poorly maintained gardens, by now in a general state of neglect. Lady

Lady Warwick took less interest in them as she became increasingly strange and eccentric, wandering around the grounds in her Edwardian finery with a rather 'other worldly' manner.20

21 The Pond and Balustrade in the Gardens at Easton Lodge

The atmosphere at Easton Lodge was always informal, with the peacocks freely strutting up and down the terrace, their cries interrupting the political discussions. The accommodation was quite basic, some of the beds were damp and rooms had to be shared. The meals were occasionally large and luxurious, but at other times scarce or non-existent. Yet the fresh air and relaxed atmosphere seemed to encourage enthusiasm for new socialist plans among the participants, who included Clement Attlee, Hugh Dalton, Hugh Gaitskill and Ernest Bevin chairing the group. The Fabian Research Bureau, which emerged from these discussions, was intended to be a permanent policy ginger-group with Clement Attlee in the chair, and G.D.H. Coleas secretary assisted by Gaitskill. When the Labour government fell in 1931, and the National Coalition was formed under Ramsay MacDonald and Baldwin, an added impetus was given to the work of the Bureau. A series of conferences were held at Easton Lodge in the early 1930s on a wide range of issues including foreign policy, agriculture and the planned economy, which helped to lay the ground for 1945 Labour Party manifesto.21

Ramsay MacDonald was also an occasional guest at Rodmarton Manor, near Cirencester. This beautiful Arts and Crafts house was built for Margaret and Claude Biddulph, a wealthy stockbroker, and they were determined to invite an eclectic mix of guests to their country house weekends. Margaret, with Quaker principles, was concerned to make the house a shrine to the principles of the movement and a center of simple living according to the principles of Ruskin and Morris. She was deeply opposed to the machine age, and wanted to give opportunities in the building of the house, its gardens and furnishing for traditional crafts such as wood carving, stone dressing and needlework. The Biddulph's was attracted by the simple life in which everyone in the local community could live together practicing their crafts in cooperative harmony.22

They took up residence in 1915 when the eastern section was completed. The large reception rooms in the middle of the house used for holding woodwork classes, basket weaving and embroidery. In the 1920s there were theatrical and musical evenings at which madrigals and folk-songs were sung, and puppet performances held for the local children. The walls were hung with hangings showing scenes from social life that were embroidered by local women of the village under the supervision of Hilda Sexton, who later went on to work of Heal's. The rugs in the corridor were by a local farm-hand, simple, rustic and beautiful. The gardens provided all the fruit and vegetables for the kitchen, and Margaret even ground her own flour. These principles of self-sufficiency and community life, and the revival of rural crafts and employment, found admirers on the Left, who were among the visitors.

These progressive-minded guests were no doubt happy to have the opportunity to live the simple life amid such beautiful surroundings, enjoying the home-grown food and rustic entertainment. However, the Biddulph's had no desire to transform society politically, or upset the social order. They were the landowners, and the Manor had all the modern conveniences of electricity and central heating, absent in the cottages of the local people in the village. Who invariably had to make do with outdoor privies. They were idealists who wanted to use their wealth and patronage to encourage rural self-sufficiency and the revival of local arts and crafts, and in this respect they shared the same views as many socialists of the time.

The influence of the aristocracy and landed gentry was in decline

22 Rodmarton Manor, Gloucestershire

between the wars, and many had difficulty maintaining their houses, and yet stately homes existed as symbols of social inequality and injustice in the countryside. Among some on the Left there was the hope that they could be taken over and used at the disposal of the people, while others wanted to see them reduced to rubble. But most hoped they might be purchased and used by public organizations, after the nationalization of land was achieved. These houses and their gardens might properly be preserved for public use, and the Workers Travel Association had already set an example. It had purchased or rented big houses for their summer visitors in the 1920s, such as East Dean at Ventor Isle of Wight. The sentiment of the WTA was that these great houses were built by the workers of previous generations who could never have afforded to stay in them, so the WTA was taking its revenge on their behalf.23

There were a few owners of great houses who showed how things could be re-ordered in a more just and equable manner. Apart from

Lady Warwick, these included Gavin Henderson who made Buscot Park in Oxfordshire available to the Fabian Society for the holding of conferences and weekend schools and who later donated it to the National Trust. Noel Buxton donated his house, Paycockes, to the Trust in 1920, and other owners tried to create model estates by turning them into communities run for the benefit of those who worked or visited them.

This was the aim of Sir Charles Trevelyan, who placed Wallington Hall and its estate in Northumberland at the disposal of the public in 1928.He was another ex-Liberal who had become a socialist convert, and Labour MP for Newcastle Upon Tyne Central between 1922 and 1931. The house was in a state of considerable neglect when he and his wife Molly set about its repair and restoration, with the aim of making the center of a community. The cottages were upgraded for the estate workers, and paid holidays and child allowances introduced. During the first summer after the restoration work was completed, Trevelyan opened the house to visitors free of charge on every weekend and public holiday, and enjoyed giving personal guided tours.24

The work at Wallington Hall continued through the years of the second Labour government of 1929-31 in which Trevelyan served as Minister of Education. He fought to raise the school leaving age, to break down sectarian barriers and make university entry accessible to all young people of talent irrespective of their means. But he found Westminster life increasingly frustrating, especially the reluctance of MacDonald to introduce socialist policies. He resigned and did not hesitate to attack the prime minister openly for political timidity, and was not too upset when he lost his seat in 1931. Later, Trevelyan was invited by the miners to stand as the Labour candidate at Morpeth but declined, writing to his wife:

What we are doing is much more worthwhile than those days of easy politics. Yet I don't regret anything. It would have been better if we had been given a job like Wallington earlier to get our teeth into. But we are learning and now – well I hope that we are entering upon a new period.....I am still not nearly content we make of Wallington. I want to try more definitely to make it a resort for socialist and internationally minded people.25

Through the 1930s and into the post-war years, Trevelyan and his wife invited both socialist and non-socialist groups as well as individuals to make use of the Wallington, so much so that it became a centre in the North East for young people who were interested in community politics. After the meetings there were the estate grounds to enjoy with walks, rambles, picnics, and joining in the continuing work of restoration and maintenance.

Wallington Hall was placed at the disposal of the Youth Hostels Association, with members regularly enjoying the accommodation and facilities. As part of its socialist mission, many adult education courses were held there, and cultural activities flourished. The Trevelyan's were keen supporters of the Arts, and Charles was appointed honorary President of the People's Theatre which had been founded in the North East in 1911. Its aim was to produce plays with social comment such as Shaw and Chekhov, with young amateur actors drawn from the region. In 1936 they performed a production of Shaw's *Candide,* with the playwright himself present.26

Although Trevelyan was expelled from the Labour Party in 1939 for promoting the popular peace front to replace the National Coalition government, he remained a committed socialist and devoted himself to running the estate. The People's Theatre continued their visits after the war, and every Whitsun Bank Holiday members were invited to go up for the weekend in groups. They slept in the bedrooms and attics of the huge old house, dined in the Great Hall and spent the days going for glorious walks, and enjoying open-air drama classes on the lawns. There was encouragement to take part in folk dancing with Lady Trevelyan giving enthusiastic directions, while accompanying the dancers on the piano.27

The Trevelyan's subscribed to the view that rural life and country pursuits added an extra dimension to the socialist cause, worked out through communal involvement and co-operative living. The house and estate at Wallington provided a refuge from the distractions of urban life, and provided the opportunity for young people to live out some of their principles in practice, albeit in a country house that was a symbol of class and power. Trevelyan believed in a community of people living and working together in a country setting, using Wallington for a purpose that was not intended. The visitors could see a 'model' working estate producing its own food, practicing craft skills, with everyone happily working together. In 1941 the house and estate were given to the National Trust, subject only to a life interest for the Trevelyan family. Charles was always ready to show visitors around the house or estate up until his death in 1958, and to show off the beautiful border countryside.28

The Elmhirst's were also concerned with creating a community at Dartington with its estates and farms, with the Hall accommodating not only the school but also an arts and craft center dedicated to producing high quality work in a communal manner. When they purchased the house and estate in 1925, there were two existing farms, Burton Farm and Skinners Bridge, and the former had to be relocated to make more room for the educational activity they envisaged. They had anew farmhouse built, designed by Alfred Fincham in 1927, and new farm buildings were added later that year with four new cottages completed in May 1927. In October 1926 the Parsonage Farm was started with new fields created and farm buildings with four new cottages completed in May 1931. The accommodation for the estate workers was of a high standard, and an improvement made in their wages and conditions of employment. There were new orchards planted, nurseries, re-forestation undertaken, and poultry introduced. They were all maintained to the highest standards of modern farming, and meant to set an example of modern agricultural planning for the rural economy.

To many socialists, being in the countryside seemed more conducive for the purposes of political education, and led to real understanding of what socialism was about. Being surrounded with the beauty and atmosphere of parkland, gardens and lakes provided keener insights into the iniquities of urban capitalism, and a contrast between them and the free gifts of nature of which every citizen should be heir. The fact that so much land, power and influence that went with it, were in the hands of so few added to the sense of moral indignation. This was added to by the conviction of many socialists that people's talents and creativity could be better fostered in rural surroundings. Those that returned to their dreary suburban lives after a visit to the country would be energized, perhaps to campaign more vigorously for change and reform. If not, they will have been inspired to live a better life and better equipped to resist the materialistic diversions of capitalist society.

7 RAMBLING AND CAMPING

With the upsurge in interest in rural life and landscape between the wars there was increased popularity in rambling and camping as the means of accessing the countryside. There was also a concern about protecting people's rights of access in the face of the increased vigilance of landlords and their agents in asserting private property rights, and restricting such access. This took the form of fencing-in land, and denying walkers and hikers rights to use traditional footpaths which may have previously been accessible for hundreds of years. At the same time there was a revival of interest in conserving the landscape and protecting it from commercial spoliation such as housing and factory overspill, new roads, leisure tourism and motorized transport both commercial and private.

The connection between good health, spiritual refreshment and physical activity in the countryside was behind the socialist promotion of hiking, cycling, canoeing and particularly rambling, perhaps the most politicized of all. In the 1890s the Glasgow Rambling Club aimed to unite 'the pleasures of a summer Saturday country ramble and the dull slogging work of socialist propaganda.' The members armed themselves with socialist songbooks, camera apparatus, a rambler's banner and literature. They would then tramp around the Lanarkshire countryside campaigning for a socialist society, and a time when 'leisure and pleasure shall be free'.[1]

Getting out into the countryside for a ramble was seen as an excellent substitute for an unhealthy and sedentary urban lifestyle, including smoking, gambling and alcohol, and was seen by some 'as the shortest cut out of Manchester.'[2] The pre-war Clarion movement had included rambling among its activities, and the Sheffield Clarion Ramblers club was formed in 1900 with the motto 'A Rambler is a Man Improved.' The club placed an advert in the *Clarion* calling for companions to go on a ramble around Kinder Scout in Derbyshire, and this had grown into a regular weekend excursion by 1902.[3]

These ramblers faced considerable opposition from the landowners and prosecutions were common, with fines and even imprisonment. The Sheffield Clarion Ramblers were obstructed with obstacles placed across their path, so they could not cross freely over the moors. Landowners were fencing off their land, and instructing agents and gamekeepers to use force to keep ramblers out. They were often armed with sticks and guns and threatened physical violence or prosecution.4 In 1896 there was a mass trespass organized on the moors outside Bolton when the land was sold to a Colonel Armstrong, who wanted to cultivate it for shooting game birds. He tried to prevent members of the public from using rightsof way over his land, andan estimated 10,000 people turned up for the mass trespass at Winter Hill. They were confronted by a phalanx of policemen and keepers, but the crowd pressed forward and pushed the police aside to pass through.5

Several prominent figures on the Left were associated with rambling, including Ramsay MacDonald, who recommended it to all comrades as part of a socialist education. He regarded rambling in the country as a corrective to his Westminster life and a means of escape. After the 1924 general election, when he became prime minister, MacDonald went walking in the hills to forget his parliamentary troubles.6It gave him a sense of perspective and surveying the beauty of a sunset in Morayshire, economic and political problems became merely 'dark ripples on the surface of things' and no longer of great importance.7

He shared the view current on the Left that appreciation of nature, with all its complexity and force, allowed people to live and cope better with modern life, 'amid the green of budding corn, the white of cherry blossoms and fleecy clouds, and the gay blue of the sky.'8 This was not simply escapism but a way of renewing his political beliefs, as socialists believed there was a connection between the beauties of the natural world and progressive politics. The forces of democratic socialism benefited from being revived and refreshed, fortified to face the rigors of political campaigning. The road to socialism was comparable to the road of a pilgrim 'mounting the hills and beyond the horizon, winds towards the ideal.'9

Many other notable figures on the Left were enthusiastic ramblers and hikers, such as G.D.H Cole and Hugh Dalton, but an even more eloquent supporter was the popular philosopher, broadcaster and writer, Cyril Joad. He had been an enthusiastic hiker since childhood, and by the 1930s was part of the movement which sought to enlarge the notion of 'Englishness' in which the landscape helped to cement a sense of belonging, and extend this to the urban working-classes. He had started serious rambling with fellow Fabians, tramping 'through the beech woods about Chorleywood, or the chalk hills near Wendover' discussing socialism on the way.10 Joad was also a supporter of the self-improving effects of rambling, both physical and spiritual, as a healthy simple way to spend leisure time well away from modern consumerism. The proponents of the new rural consciousness sought to re-define the traditional English concern for the landscape as unsullied and therefore representative of solid English virtue. As part of this, the working class had the same rights to enjoy rural amenities as the wealthy, and on a free and equal basis. This campaign was a struggle of practical socialism in action, with the added advantage of helping to raise the political consciousness of working people.

The other strand of this revived interest in rural life and landscape grew out of an increasing awareness that it was under threat, and needed protection and conservation. The aim was to prevent further commercial spoliation, and encroachment of modern life into the still un-spoilt countryside. This movement included people of all political persuasions or none, but on the left it particularly fitted in with its belief in the non-exclusivity of rural life and access, and need to resist ever more powerful commercial forces so evident in the 1930s. These included urban overspill, unplanned housing sprawl, pylons, aerodromes, military firing ranges, reservoirs, the ever greater volume of traffic, and advertising hoardings. Another threat was the re-styling of leisure around motorized transport: coaches, cars and motor-bikes with side-cars, so that 'speed was no longer the purpose but instead a diversion from the main highways in search of beauty'.11

Although based in London during the week, Cyril Joad escaped whenever possible to his favourite haunts on the Sussex Downs. Occasionally he rented a cottage for weekends and holidays, but more often took the train or bus with rucksack and stout walking boots to ramble across southern and eastern England or further afield. In time he hoped to become a small-holder and practice the ideals of rural self-sufficiency and democratic husbandry, an ambition he achieved in the 1940s, although quite a disillusioning experience. On his rambles, Joad became alarmed at what he saw as the encroachment of modern life on country vistas that had been unspoilt, and was one of the first to warn about the consequences. He castigated suburban sprawl, litter, debris, new roads, roadhouses, mobile cafes and other blights of modern life a she saw it. It was like being a living witness, he felt, to a changing landscape and wrote about the many eye-sores such as the estates of new bungalows, advertising hoardings or some other 'shouting pink horror,' that were not only inherently ugly, but erected without the slightest care for their effect for the environment.12

Already familiar with the Lake District, North Wales, and the West Country, Joad began exploring rural Essex, a favourite county for progressive-minded socialists and idealists. Taking the train from Liverpool Street station deep into the county, he would change from the main line at Colchester or Chelmsford and alight at some isolated stop and start walking. In this way he discovered that Essex was not as flat and featureless as many supposed, and climbing a little hill he saw the countryside spread out like an enormous picture. The spacing and shape of trees gave them a special significance, each distinct in form and individuality; three or more together in solitary groups in empty fields, brooding presences in the landscape.13

At the time the Essex countryside, as in much of rural England, gave a semi-deserted impression, and the winding roads often ended abruptly at a solitary abandoned farm. It was a shock to Joad to discover these farms with their white-washed walls left deserted and derelict, and to find the countryside so lovely and yet so completely unoccupied and uncared-for. Wheat-farming had collapsed and nothing much was left except the immense skyline, and when that was reached another empty landscape beyond. There had once been fully productive farms in these spaces, and a whole community of farmers and farm workers in the now abandoned villages. The message was clear: the need to revive agriculture and return the people to the land that had once been worked for generations. In this way life could be brought back to a landscape, but this time organized on more equable and cooperative lines.14

The denial of public access to the countryside led to an increasingly vocal campaign in the 1930s as thousands were joining rambling and

and cycling clubs, eager to escape at weekends and holiday times from the working world of office and factory. The conflict between the desire of these people to reach the wildest and least accessible parts of the countryside, and the landowners who wanted to keep them out, soon revived. The landowners were fencing in their properties, and becoming increasingly litigious in pursuing their legal rights, and many were well-resourced commercial companies.

The campaign for right of access involved thousands of people, mainly in the North where the issue had long been highly contentious. Cyril Joad was anxious to do all he could to voice the ramblers grievances to wider audience at the time he was becoming well-known as a writer, polemical journalist, broadcaster and public controversialist. Holding strong views about the iniquities of 'landlordism' and unchecked commercialism, he was concerned about the balance of nature being upset, and believed strongly in education of the public to mobilize them to combat it. He had inherited the old socialist belief in self-improvement through leisure, but wanted a concerted effort made to educate the users of the countryside so they were more responsible in their behavior.

The coach tours taking thousands of urban working-class day trippers into the countryside did not meet with his approval, and were seen as another threat. A large number of coach companies were formed in the 1930s, operating year round excursions from city centers to a wide range of destinations. They were cheap and cheerful, and the 'charabanc' excursion soon became a popular way for the working class to enjoy day out. There were also trips organized by works social committees, and working men's clubs, to such popular venues as the Lake District, the Derbyshire Dales and the Sussex Downs. There were frequent stops made at pubs and roadhouses along the way, with food and drink consumed by passengers during breaks on the journey and when they arrived on the beach or in a field. There were also communal singing on the coach, jokes and banter with a good deal of noise.

Such unrestricted populist tourism was anathema to high-minded socialists and conservationists such as Joad and others, and created a conflict between their views on public access and the need for regulation and instruction. They believed that access to nature and landscape must be part of a educative process, with unregulated mass tourism part of the problem. There were also concerns about the threats by mass tourism to un-spoilt villages and the effects on country paths through over-use, the threat to wildlife and natural habitats. They understood the countryside did not remain static over time, and had always evolved in proportion to essential human needs, such as the need to avoid starvation, rather than greed or profit.15While rural incursions by ramblers, cyclists and campers, were approved because they made little permanent impact on the countryside, and were easier to regulate, educate and organize. They could claim to have a self-improving purpose, and many of the ramblers clubs made this explicit in their mission statements.

The Youth Hostel Association, founded in April 1930 shared these self-improving ideals. Its objectives were 'to help all, especially young people of limited means, to a greater knowledge, love and access of the countryside, particularly by providing hostels or other simple accommodation for them in their travels, and to promote their health, rest and education.'15 With the explicit aim of encouraging greater understanding of the countryside as well as providing cheap accommodation, the YHA saw itself as having a social purpose shared by many on the Left. It was not politically aligned, although the Labour Party affiliated to it on behalf of the Labour League of Youth, and approved its values.

The YHA sought to promote healthy bodies and minds and in pursuing this to facilitate freedom of the countryside. It wanted to develop responsible values through experience of a more simple and basic lifestyle. This chimed very much with the socialist view that the unspoilt nature of the countryside was morally superior and healthier than urban life. It also fitted well with the preservationist movement that sought to limit the effect of modern commercial pressures to the rural environment. From its earliest years the YHA did not encourage motorists, and this was made clear in the YHA Handbook :

> Hostels are intended for Members when walking or cycling, and are not open to motorists or motor cyclists (unless they are using the hostels for the purposes of walking or climbing…..16

The first YHA hostel was opened at Llanwrst in North Wales in October 1930, but it soon closed because of problems with the water supply. However, further hostels were soon opened and by the end of 1931 there were seventy-one open, even though some closed due to lack of demand which made them financially unviable.17 The great majority remained popular and prospered, partly due to the low prices of 1/- per night's stay for over 25's and 6d for junior members under 25. An annual membership was offered of 5/- shillings for seniors and 2/6 for juniors, which was good value. The hostels themselves were rather spartan, offering simple but adequate accommodation for an overnight stay, with separate dormitories for men and women.18A warden was in charge of each hostel, some of which provided inexpensive meals while most had self-catering facilities.

23 YHA Hostel at Thorney How, Grasmere, Cumbria in the 1930s

The YHA was divided into regions responsible for the management of the hostels within its borders, and in 1935 there were 19 regions with a National Office located significantly in Welwyn Garden City.19 To stay at a hostel a rambler or cyclist had to be a member of the YHA, and the cooperative spirit was encouraged by expecting all members to contribute to the running of the hostels during their stay. They would undertake a range of duties as cleaning, washing-up and carrying water, if there was a piped supply. A strong communal ethos was reflected and reinforced in the dormitories, common rooms and cooking arrangements. This provided an extension to the cooperative spirit found in rambling and cycling groups who were the main occupants. By 1939 there were 297 youth hostels across Britain with 83,000 members ad 600,000 overnight stays in that year alone.20

The YHA soon became an essential element in the outdoor life of many ramblers, cyclists and campers, and was highly valued. Many socialists were enthusiastic supporters from the outset, including Cyril Joad who saw it as a way of encouraging more people to enjoy the outdoor rural life, in the structured way of which he approved. Always willing to give talks to members and speak on its behalf, he was also invited, as well-known personality, to open new hostels. In the winter of 1933 he spoke to the Lakeland group of the YHA, pleading the case for wider access to the mountains and 'national parks.' He took the opportunity of criticizing Lord Lonsdale, a local landowner, for defending property and sporting rights in a recently published book. Joad castigated all attempts to ban people from the land, especially if it was to provide facilities for the wealthy to kill wild-life. He urged all landowners to allow more rights of way and wider access to their land, while encouraging walkers and ramblers to use it responsibly. The speech was intentionally provocative, and the next day's headlines obligingly screamed 'LORD LONSDALE ATTACKED.' The newspapers alleged that Joad had urged walkers to pull down private property notices, leave gates open and pull down fences. In fact, he had urged landowners to do these things themselves and for ramblers to behave with restraint.21

The tradition of campaigning for walkers rights in the North was revived in the 1930s by ramblers groups. They were mainly young, idealistic, and often committed socialists, some of whom had moved to the city seeking work from rural conditions which were worse. Most of them were, however, born and bred in cities such as Manchester and Sheffield, the main centres of urban-based ramblers. They enjoyed getting out of the grimy city every weekend to breath fresh air in a cleaner and healthier environment of the moors and dales, only a few miles away. Finding themselves denied access to these beautiful landscapes, they began to be more vocal in demanding Guaranteed freedom of access and the designation of footpaths that followed ancient rights of way. They campaigned for the creation of National Parks in areas of special natural beauty, such as the Derbyshire Peak District.

The campaigns and protests became more radical, and there was a mass trespass at Winnats Pass in the Peak District, organized by the Sheffield Ramblers. This was followed in April 1932 by a mass trespass at Kinder Scout by Manchester ramblers with strong influence from the communist dominated British Workers Sports Federation. It was a genuinely popular expression of anger at denial of access to the moors. The BWSF had already organized mass rallies of ramblers and cyclists accompanied with speeches and communal singing, and open air sketches performed by the workers theatre movement.22

24 Part of the Kinder Scout Mass Trespass, April 1932

At Kinder Scout several protestors were arrested, with five found guilty by magistrates and jailed for between two and five months. Among the magistrates were a brigadier, three captains, two majors, two aldermen, and eleven country landowners, so the convictions could be portrayed in class terms. Many saw the verdicts as a result of the inevitable conflict between vested landed interests protected by the law, and the rights of the majority who were excluded from accessing their own country.23 The event became part of Northern rambling folklore, commemorated to-day at the site where a blue plaque in the rock was unveiled in 1982 by Benny Rothman, one of the leaders. It is remembered in the lyrics of the 'Manchester Rambler', written soon after the event by Ewan MacColl, which became the theme song of the Ramblers Association. Even though the RA was founded by politically non-aligned rambling organization, the chorus of the song makes its political message clear:

> I'm a rambler, I'm a rambler, down Manchester way
> I do my rambling the hard moorland way
> I may be a wage slave on Monday
> But I am a free man on Sunday

However, many ramblers were non-political, and there were concerns from some quarters about the politicization of the activity, especially as youth movements in Europe were becoming an evident feature of the far-right political scene. But militant ramblers felt it was necessary to break the law and show how unjust it was, and to attract publicity for the cause. For years they had been harried by gamekeepers employed by the landowners to preserve the grouse on their land, as well as land agents for the water companies who owned land, and adding insult to the injury of flooding beautiful valleys for reservoirs. Ramblers thought they were faced with vested interests on one kind or another, which made the campaign for access and rights of way inevitably political.

This was also the view of Cyril Joad, who took a delight in leading gamekeepers a merry dance over the moors. When confronted by them he would criticize what they were doing, and try to confront them with the ethics of their actions. At the time, the influence of game sports was extensive across the country including the Peak District, and ramblers believed it should be stopped. Many thought it ridiculous that only those prepared to kill wild life had the right of access to the moors and valleys.

Many ramblers shared the view that the campaign for public access to the land was part of the struggle for full democratic rights, and the trespass laws should not impede this struggle for civil rights, that had in any case been overturned by the sovereign will of the majority. The campaign adopted this radical tone especially in the North, and with more resonance at a time when the political culture in Britain seemed one of drift and torpor. The sight of hundreds, sometimes thousands, of ramblers from different classes and backgrounds demonstrating to obtain rural rights cheered many observers on the left. Cyril Joad, for example, addressed large open-air meetings of radicalized ramblers before they set off to put into practice his exhortation to take back their rights as free men and women.24

In 1934 the Rights of Way Act was passed, partly due to all this pressure, but was soon seen by ramblers as woefully inadequate. It did not create new footpaths, but merely recognized those that already existed. More vigilant policing was encouraged by designating footpaths, to ensure no one strayed off them, which led to further intimidation of ramblers. The cause was still not won, and they perhaps needed a coherent manifesto around which they could coalesce. To some extent this was provided by *A Charter for Ramblers,* written by Cyril Joad as a polemic arguing the case for the comprehensive rights of ramblers, and linking their cause with a demand for protection of the countryside. He argued that it was just as important to preserve the landscape they wanted to enjoy, before it was too late. Each generation was morally bound to hand on 'undefiled to posterity as an instrument, the most important we possess, for the training of citizens of the future in the art of living.'25 Although inclined to be didactic, and at times patronizing towards the 'people' and their rights, Joad was not alone in taking this view of rural Britain as a backdrop for civil education. He saw this education of the citizens of the future as a priority, so they could enjoy their leisure constructively, and provide a bulwark against future despoliation. The aim was to preserve the rural environment so that each generation could live in harmony with nature on an equal basis, without imposing excess human pressure upon it. This view challenged the notion of a landscape that could be preserved with all the existing rights and privileges remaining intact, handed down through successive generations of a privileged elite with all its inequalities.26

In 1934 there was a further demonstration at Winnats Pass organized by the Manchester and District Ramblers Federation, one of the more radical campaigning group. In his speech to the assembled ramblers Cyril Joad praised the way in which young people were discovering for themselves the joys of the countryside, and how walking in it was showing them new ways in which to live their lives. This he contrasted with the hypocrisy of so-called 'sportsmen' who slaughter the wildlife with the help of their gamekeepers, who seemed to spend their time trying to find ways to harass ramblers. He reiterated the demand for 'National Parks' to be created as areas of designated natural beauty, with the Peak District as a prime example.

The rambling groups came together in 1935 to form the Ramblers Association. Some of the members, including socialists, hoped it would carry forward on a national level the demands of ramblers. They wanted to campaign on a wide front that included the protection of the countryside from commercial exploitation and road transport. In this respect, the RA soon disappointed them, seeming to be more interested in organizing rambles and campaigning for cheaper rail travel for members. Typical was the 'Walking Ticket Tours' programme by which ramblers could alight at one country station, compete a ramble, and depart home from another station. Most members were happy with this kind of initiative, but wanted it to go further and to be bolder. They still regarded the farmers and landowners as the enemy who were generally right-wing, underpaid their workers, and were set on denying the people their democratic rights. But the majority on the RA executive disagreed, and were intent on limiting activities to lobbying government and landlords, careful to appear respectable and respectful of the law.

There was, therefore, a tension between the more militant ramblers, generally on the Left, and the more moderate who believed in respecting the law and could not condone trespassing as a form of protest. Cyril Joad was contemptuous of the latter, dismissing them as looking and dressing like ramblers, speaking interminably about the joys of rambling, but unwilling to risk anything to claim their rights of access to the countryside. To many socialists, deeply entrenched vested interests never gave up their rights until forced to do so. Using persuasion, showing how respectable and law abiding ramblers could be would have no effect, and only direct action would keep the issues alive and force change.27

The growth in country pursuits, such as rambling and cycling, went with an increase in camping under canvas between the wars. Previously, camping had largely been a middle-class activity after being first popularized by Thomas Hiram Holding. He saw that the increase in bicycle ownership meant the middle classes could go off camping, and designed a special lightweight tent for them. He also set up the Association of Cycle Campers in 1906, and published the *Campers Handbook* in 1908, which contained all kinds of practical advice on selecting camp sites, pitching of tents, camp-fire cooking and so on. Going camping was a fashionable activity for a time among middle-class Oxbridge undergraduate students, including Fabians such as the Evan Durbin, High Dalton, and John Strachey, and those on the fringes of the Bloomsbury group.28

Camping became increasingly popular with the working-class, not least because it was cheap and did not require expensive equipment. It was also popular on the Left because it was an unpretentious and communal form of open-air activity, perhaps the best means to get close to nature. The political philosopher G.A. Cohen, in his book *Why Not Socialism?* used camping as a metaphor to argue the case for a wider socialist society. He argued that it requires a high level of sharing and caring, rather than acquisitiveness and selfishness. Each member of the camp may have special talents, for example cooking, fishing, or putting up tents, but these talents can be put at the service of the whole group. The camp provides equality of opportunity and a reduction in inequalities of social disadvantage, and natural physical or intellectual disadvantages are eliminated. Instead, a sense of communalism prevails as competition is counter-productive and undermines the success of the joint-enterprise. A successful camp requires all its participants to practice the camping virtues of trust, unselfishness and unity.29 If these virtues can be successfully practiced in camping why not in the wider society:

> Our common aim is that each of us should have a good time, doing so as far as possible, the things he or she does best (some of those things we do together, others we do separately) We have facilities with which to carry out our enterprise, for example, pots and pans, oil, coffee, fishing rods...30

This kind of thinking was common between the wars, when 'camping with a purpose' became more widespread among all social groups and organizations. But the Left realized the usefulness of combining the co-operative and communal nature of the group, with the function of political education. This propaganda element of camping had already been applied successfully by Baden Powell in the Scouting movement, where the camp became an almost ritualized event developing its own traditions and rituals, permitting the more effective transmission of values that the leadership wanted absorbed by the members. The groups which broke away from Scouting, Kibbo Kift and the Woodcraft Folk, were both broadly leftwing in orientation, and contemptuous of what they saw as the militaristic nature of the Scouting movement. And yet they both used the camp and camping in the same way, and adopted their own rituals for a different purpose.

Another more permanent camp set up in the 1930s was the Grith Fyrd camps for unemployed men. This radical alternative educational movement set up two work camps, at Godshill in Hampshire and at Shining Cliff in Derbyshire with no more than fifty members in each. The idea behind the camps was to provide unemployed men with the opportunity to create a land-based settlement, based largely on their labour and self-sufficient, by exchanging goods and services with each other. It was founded by the order of Woodcraft Chivalry which was influenced by Ernest Thompson Seton whose views, based on observation of native Indian culture in the North America, was a mixture of socialism, co-operation and anti-urbanism. These were all present in the Grith Fyrd camps, together with a strong feeling of internationalism and pacifism. A further aim of Grith Fyrd, which means 'Peace Army' in Old English, was to combat the exploitation of labour, and its materialist distractions, by providing opportunities for young people to express their creativity and self-expression.[31]

Another underlying aim was to expose camp members to the natural world by living life on a basic level, so making self-reliance easier and minimizing the influence of the decadence in modern society. The camp members were mainly unemployed working-class men, who were drawing the dole, mixed with middle class idealists. Living mainly in tents which they erected themselves, they also built the furniture and grew their own food. One of the camps was visited by Pathe News cameras, and the film shows the spartan living conditions, including washing in the river and communal eating.[32]

The camps were admired by several left-wing intellectuals, such as Aldous Huxley, for their attempt to go back to rural open-air primitivism, and as a way of combating the standardization and alienation of modern life. They also admired the leisure activities in the camps, redolent of earlier socialist land settlements, such as Morris dancing, folk singing, and adult education classes.[33] It was an experiment in living that did not survive the 1930s, though the experiment was continued by a small number of veterans at the Braziers Hill community in the later 1940's, but it was more like a communitarian college of adult education. The camps were in some ways ahead of their time in trying to create a means of personal fulfillment for the young unemployed, and doing so in a co-operative, fraternal community which encouraged self-reliance, social responsibility, and a concern for protecting the natural environment.34

The renewed interest in open air life and in health and fitness generally during the 1930s, added to the swelling numbers of campers and camp-sites. The Labour League of Youth and the Young Communist League were enthusiastic campers under canvas, and their young members enjoyed the camaraderie and the change of scene, despite the accompanying political 'education.' But it was becoming increasingly difficult to pitch tents on private land, and more restrictions were being introduced. Some local authorities issued by-laws to prevent the erection of mobile dwellings, which included tents of a certain size. In addition, the Public Health Act of 1936 banned the sale of some food and drink on campsites, such as bread, butter and milk, limited sites to one tent per acre, and forbade tents to be within twenty-feet on a hedge.

Rambling, cycling, youth hostelling and camping were all part of the new purposeful use of leisure in the inter-war years, and popular with all kinds of people. But socialists and others on the Left adopted a purposeful involvement in these activities, with a particular enthusiasm which expressed itself in several ways. It was combined with campaigning for access to the land, for more rights of way, and the creation of designated areas of natural beauty and public education. The activities provided a lot of pleasure, keeping participants physically fit and healthy, providing a sense of purpose, and a political education. There was also the underlying conviction that exposure to scenic beauty and the wonders of nature had a refreshing effect on the human spirit, helping people to cope better with their everyday urban lives.

8 SPORT AND HOLIDAY LEISURE

For many socialists the outdoor life was celebrated through sport, which had valued since the 1890s, notably by the Clarion clubs. From that time professional football became the main working-class spectator sport, and in the summer months cricket had a large following especially in the Northern professional leagues, as well as county and test cricket. In 1909 socialist meetings in the West Riding of Yorkshire had to be cancelled because the crowd preferred to attend local football matches, and it was soon realized that it would be more effective for socialist groups to sponsor and promote popular sports rather than compete with them.1

Even before the Labour and Communist Parties decided to go down this path, independent groups of a left-wing persuasion had been formed with the purpose of organizing sport and outdoor activities. The Clarion sports clubs are an example already examined, and these continued promoting various sports until well after the First World War. Their activities were regularly reported in *The Clarion,* together with reports from professional football and cricket matches in the North.

The Clarion clubs aimed to combine the pleasures of outdoor activity with political education and propaganda, and there were other groups with the same purpose. The Ancoats Recreation Movement of Manchester was another left-leaning, but non-aligned, organization with the aim of promoting reform and the ideals of the brotherhood of man. In 1886 it formed a rambling club in the city, and in 1895 a cycling club followed by an athletics club. It organized walking tours and weekend excursions to the Lake District, and invited various Labour figures to visit and speak to its groups, including J.R. Clynes, Tom Mann, Philip Snowden and Ben Tillett.2

After 1918 trade unions and co-operative societies became involved in organizing sporting activities for their members, mostly local football teams but other sports were involved. These included the Kings Lynn Labour Sports Club, the North London Workers Union Tennis Club, and Southampton Workers Social and Athletic Club.

There were sections for boxing, athletics, as well as social entertainment and excursions to the countryside and seaside. Some of these clubs were fortunate enough to have their own sports grounds such as the Leicestershire Cooperative Society which had a cricket pitch, tennis courts, bowling green and football pitches all with changing rooms.3

When the British Workers Sports Federation was established in April 1923 by a group of Labour Party activists, it provided a national organization which had the potential to co-ordinate all this local activity. The BWSF was founded largely under the auspices of the Labour Party, the Co-operative movement and the Clarion Cycling Clubs with the aim of promoting working-class sport, including at international level, to 'further the causes of peace among nations.'4 The hope was that international sports meetings between workers across Europe would promote both fraternity and peace, increase understanding by substituting sporting values for nationalistic ones.5

The BWSF was quite successful in encouraging sports activities, although whether this led to increased political activism is doubtful. But the membership figures of some branches was impressive, over a thousand members in the Glasgow branch, while the London branch made contacts with trade unions, the ILP and local Labour Party branch members. It organized Gala Days, which included tug of war contests, one mile walks, and a ladies 'thread and needle races.'6 Some branches were more active than others, and the London branch sponsored tours of Germany. In 1927 the Trades Union Congress officially sponsored the BWSF, and this led to participation in the Workers Olympiad in Prague in 1927. Despite this, the BWSF was not as influential or active as the hundreds of independent local clubs such as the Gorton ILP Rambling Club or the Willesden Socialist Cycling Club in London, and the Printing and Allied Trades Amateur Boxing Club.

The British Communist Party (CPGB) also saw the political advantages of promoting sport and physical fitness to influence its members, and through them to the wider society. The party view was that physical fitness was necessary to perform effectively, and withstand the ravages of the capitalist system. The aim was to create a legion of young workers for whom sport and exercise played a crucial role in forming an organic whole with their political education. It was assumed that mental and physical education went together, and were an excellent advertisement for the communist way of life.7

In Newcastle and Scotland boxing was popular and well-organized by the party with exhibition bouts, and in Manchester rambling and camping were highly popular. There were football leagues in London, Glasgow, South Wales and Derby as well as the CP cycling clubs such Spartacus and the Red Wheelers. In Essex the party held an annual camp at Clacton-on-Sea, and the Hackney club organized boxing and road running on Thursdays, rambles on Sundays, and sports meetings at High Beeches and in Victoria Park. The camps of the Young Communist League were physically strenuous, involving pitching tents, sleeping under canvas, open-air cooking and camp-fire sing-songs. At the YCL Tyneside district camp in June 1928, held at Finchale Abbey in County Durham, the campers rose at 7.30am and were expected to take part in physical exercises for an hour before cooking and eating breakfast.8

In 1930 the National Workers Sports Association was formed to encourage, promote, and control amateur sport and recreation among working-class organizations under the auspices of the TUC and the Labour Party. By 1932 it had eighteen sports bodies affiliated to it, nine district committees, one hundred and forty-five sections and 5,000 members, and by 1938 this had grown to three hundred and eighty affiliated clubs with 13,000 members. The NWSA was involved in fourteen different sports by 1935, and organized events such as netball tournaments, rowing competitions and tennis matches.

Lawn tennis was particularly popular in the summer despite its bourgeois image and exclusive private clubs. In 1927 two members of the Reading Labour Party, George Deacon and Ivy Noyes, who loved tennis decided to set up a club at which all their comrades could play. They rented part of the old Athletic Ground at Corsham, a suburb of Reading, and created our courts with nets having raised £40 in subscriptions. The Labour Party Tennis Club was founded as the first socialist tennis club in Britain. By 1932 it had 90 members and was one of the largest tennis clubs in the town. Then Deacon and Noyes decided to organize a national tennis tournament open to all. Several other local Labour Party Tennis Clubs had started around the country, and their members were invited to compete at the National

Workers Tennis Championship at Caversham and Nutley in September 1932 and was considered a great success.9

It was George Elvin, a trade union leader and leading figure in the BWSF, who decided to organize an even more ambitious tournament the next year in Reading. In 1933 there were 100 participants, and it became known as the 'Workers' Wimbledon' continuing for another twenty years in various locations such as Brockwell Park in South London and at Southsea. The *Portsmouth Evening News* described the participants as 'railwaymen, woodworkers, clerks, shop assistants, bank clerks and insurance men…..all ordinary working people and quite a number of them never had a minutes coaching in their lives. Their tennis has been snatched after hours hurriedly and the result is surprisingly good.' George Elvin's rationale for the tournament was clear, seeing sport as ' but an aid to the development of body and mind. Our best player soften sacrifice practice for work in the Labour cause.' Sport, therefore, helped to make better comrades and more effective workers in the struggle for socialism.10

The actual Wimbledon Men's Final was won three times in the 1930s by Fred Perry, who became enormously popular with the public. He was born in a terraced house in Stockport, the son of Stan F. Perry, socialist and secretary of the Cooperative Party. The tennis world at the time was entirely amateur, with most of the players and officials from the middle and upper middle-classes. Having been an outstanding table-tennis player, Perry switched to tennis at the age of 18, but was regarded at the All England Club as a working-class upstart and treated with some contempt. After winning the first of his titles the club tie, awarded to all champions, was left on a chair for him to find instead of being properly presented.11 He was a working class hero, and Perry's success led to a upsurge in interest in lawn tennis in socialist and non-socialist sports clubs, which unfortunately was not sustained after 1945. Sam, in reference to his son's success, noted that 'our pleasure is shared by co-operators throughout Britain by whom Fred is justly regarded as one of ourselves.'12

The Co-operative movement had realized early the importance and appeal of sporting activity in the open air. In 1929 the Co-operative Wholesale Society provided £10,000 for the purchase of sports facilities and grounds at Batley, Birmingham, Hebden Bridge, Leicester, Liverpool, and Manchester among other places. All sports were catered for, and local Co-op stores and factories organized teams and competitions. The Co-op Longsight Printing Works in Manchester had its own cricket team, swimming, and tennis clubs, while the Silvertown Co-op factory in the East End London docklands set up a social and athletic committee, which organized a similar range of sports. All over the country there were similar Co-op sports activities in places as various at Avonmouth Flour Mills which had an athletic club, and the Newcastle Boot and Shoe Department which fielded football and cricket teams. By 1932 the London Co-operative Society Engineers Sports Club had a membership of 6,900 and a superb sports ground at Chingford laid out for a range of sports.13

Several leading Labour figures, notably George Lansbury, supported the National Playing Fields Association, founded in 1925 which continued adding to its acquisitions of sports facilities throughout the 1930s. Although non-political with royal patronage and government support, the Labour Party was represented on the governing body. The NPFA sought to provide the unemployed and working poor with the means to play sport by providing open spaces for football and cricket pitches and other sports, and also by making available equipment such as cricket and football gear, golf clubs, hockey sticks. The work of the NPFA supplemented the provision of open air sports facilities by local authorities, many controlled by Labour and patronized by the working class who could not afford fees to join private clubs. The 'six acre standard' recommended by the NAPF was generally adopted by many local authorities when providing play areas on housing developments, and public playing fields. These facilities ranged from football and cricket pitches in the local parks, tennis courts, lakes stocked with fish for angling and municipal golf courses.

Although the motivation of the socialists and communists in encouraging open air sport were different, they both shared the ideal of encouraging wider working-class participation. They also hoped outdoor sport would be a corrective to the physical jobs most working-class people did, often in unhealthy working conditions. Playing sport, preferably outdoors in a healthy atmosphere, also encouraged co-operation and fraternity, which led to greater class unity and solidarity. But there was also a suspicion on the left of the amateur sports establishment, with its strong overtones of social class hierarchy and militarism. Providing sports facilities for their working-class membership offset, to some extent, the privileges of the amateurs in their private sports clubs. The sports fields and equipment socialist clubs, local authorities, and the NAPF provided, helped increase working-class levels of ability and provided recruits into the professional ranks of several sports, notably association football and county cricket.14

The inter-war years saw a boom in the construction of lidos or open air swimming pools. A few of these had been constructed before 1918, but many more were built in the 1930's, several in Labour-controlled authorities and by the London County Council. They were not just swimming pools, but in many cases extremely impressive community 'leisure centers', owned and built by the local council, often in the white tiled *art modern* style fashionable at the time with modern facilities of all minds, and catering for everyone from young people to couples and family groups. They were extremely popular and people spent the whole day in summer eating picnics on the grassy slopes as well as swimming and diving. The LCC opened the Brockwell Lido in 1935, and others were opened at Edmonton, Tottenham, Ruislip and Rush Green between 1935-7, and in many other parts of the country including Banbury, Grange-over-Sands and Ipswich. By this time the open air movement also enjoyed the support of the government, and in 1936 the highly impressive Larks-wood Lido was opened by a government minister, Kingsley Wood, at Chingford in North London.

The self-improving effect of open air sporting activities as a diversion from materialistic values appealed to the Left, so it is not surprising that organized holidays for the workers should have had a similar appeal. Working-class leisure was hampered generally by the lack of paid holidays, impossible for many to arrange or afford, and largely the preserve of the middle-classes. Day-trips and shorter coach and rail excursions were getting more common before 1918, and seaside resorts had developed to cater for this need.

The early middle-class socialists were strongly influenced in their holiday tastes by the outdoor movement. This advocated a closeness to nature, combined with all the virtues of living a simpler life in rural surroundings. These ideas influenced those early socialist groups that set out to provide holidays for the working class. They had a disdain for the consumerism of the commercial seaside holidays, already popular with resorts such as Blackpool with its boarding houses, hotels and frivolous leisure facilities.

The *Clarion* always took an interest in the leisure activities of its readers, and regularly included reports of summer excursions and trips they had made. Typical among these was an approving account of a trip by sailing boat on the river Weaver, past grimy chemical factories, joining up with the equally dingy Manchester Ship Canal, and on to Eastham on the Mersey.15 The paper was also ready to criticize holidays of which it disapproved, such as an overcrowded railway excursion to the seaside on August Bank Holiday in 1892.15 The *Clarion* was much opposed to the increasingly commercialized seaside holiday, inevitably citing Blackpool, and considered rambling in the Derbyshire Dales, the Lake District, and other 'un-spoilt' country areas as far more edifying and self-improving.16

The Clarion Field Club encouraged the study of geology and natural history, while the Clarion Cycling Club continued promoting the virtues of peddle-power and socialism into the 1930s. Trips into the countryside were regarded as inherently laudable, and almost any activity in it seemed to be invested with a superior quality. The Clarion clubs drew like-minded people together for a range of activities, all involving fresh-air and exercise in the country. Whether day-trips, weekend, or longer excursions, they were fraternal but informal groups of people with similar socialist sympathies. Not in any way puritanical or prudish, a good deal of drinking, smoking, singing and joking took place during these outings.

A pioneer in providing a residential summer programmes of self-improvement for the working class was the National Home Reading Union. Starting in July 1889 with a summer assembly in Blackpool, it provided a break for working-class members from the numbing grind of their daily lives. Although evangelical in inspiration, it's aim was to raise the horizons of working-class people by encouraging reading circles in their communities, meeting in libraries, schoolrooms or private homes.17 An off-shoot of the NHRU was the Co-operative Holiday Association, started in 1891 to offer holidays at low cost to poor working people. Its founder and secretary, T.A. Leonard, who was also the founder and leading light of the Labour Church movement that was for a time very active and influential in some of the Northern cities. Leonard was active in the CHA as secretary and a group leader on vigorous walks and hikes, which invariably involved serious walking with rucksacks and stout boots, such as one he led in 1891 from Blackburn all the way to Ambleside in the Lake District. He tended to favour landscapes that were both hard to travel and scenically most impressive. But the aim was always self-reliance, and the use of human power rather than any commercial means of transportation, with with only the most basic accomodation provided.[18]

25 T.A. Leonard leads a walking party

But seaside holidays also held appeal so long as they were at workaday and 'unspoilt' places such as Filey or Whitby, where the CHA had its first headquarters. Another favourite location was in the Lake District which combined tranquility, impressive scenery and remoteness. At first the CHA only had a few hundred members, but it grew rapidly from 268 in 1893 to 10,719 in 1911 and 30,000 by 1914.[19]It offered simple and inexpensive holidays with fraternal fellowship spent in scenic places. This clearly had considerable appeal, and the CHA continued to both purchase and rent property as accommodation for its vacationers, each center with a leader responsible for organizing the activities.[20]

By 1913 the CHA was operating thirteen holiday centers, but with this success tensions developed between Leonard and the members of the management committee. He felt that the organization was straying from the original remit of providing cheap holidays for the working-poor, and becoming too middle class in its clientele and ethos. This included catering to middle-class standards of comfort, with all the resulting costs implications. What Leonard wanted was more youth- camps and mountain huts, and other kinds of basic accommodation, that would permit younger working-class people to enjoy an inexpensive week or so in the fresh air.21

The CHA had its own journal, *Comradeship,* in which articles appeared on such subjects as opposing mountain railways, the pollution of streams by new electrical works, and praising the magnificent views on the train journey from the western Highlands to the Kyle of Lochalsh.22 There was a sense of actual or potential loss pervading many of the articles, and nostalgia for a times which were, it was implied, preferable to the present. Some articles were prescient in their keen awareness of the threat to the rural and built environment, but also realistic about change:

> It is pleasant to think that the fair, or pretty things, the abbeys or cathedrals, the villages, old inns, wild flowers, lanes and squares of historic cities and the rest are mere legacies, really crumbling, decaying, passing away.23

One of the Co-operative Holiday Association's most popular centers was at Hebden Bridge in North Yorkshire, from where summer walks were organized to Malham and Gordale Scar among other places. These were described in *Comradeship,* with emphasis on the fellowship found among the members, all sharing the same co-operative and fraternal values, whatever their backgrounds. These holidays also provided a safe way for single women to enjoy a slightly unconventional experience which enabled them to meet other single people, and perhaps find long term friendship or companionship.24

In 1913 T.H. Leonard broke away from the CHA to form the Holiday Fellowship, which opened camps on the Isle of Sheppey in Kent, Conway in North Wales, and at Staithes in Scotland. They were mainly for children, but others were opened for families and single adults. The assumptions behind its work were the same as the CHA: that all working people needed for a good time was good fellowship spent in beautiful natural surroundings. But the Holiday Fellowship also found it difficult to reach as many sections the working class as it would have liked, such a single women and young male apprentices in skilled trades preferred seaside holidays with their mates drinking, chasing girls, and in fun-fairs and amusement arcades.25

The anti-commercialization of holidays was shared by the early holiday camps in which worker's groups were the pioneers. The first socialist holiday camp was started by John Fletcher Dodd in 1936, at Caister on the Norfolk coast. He was a member of the ILP and Clarion Cycling Club, and wanted to create a holiday atmosphere with socialist values in an camp setting. It started with only a few friends living under canvas on the seafront, but increasing numbers joined every year, and by 1911 huts and chalets had been built. There were organized events and entertainments introduced, including dancing, sports competitions, debates and lectures. Fletcher Dodd insisted a strict regime with no drinking, gambling or talking loudly after 11pm..The atmosphere was decidedly communal in intent with some campers growing their own vegetables, cooking and washing, all the domestic tasks that kept costs down and made the camp self-sufficient and affordable.26

After 1918 improving living standards meant the original aims of providing cheap and healthy holidays in the open-air, were undermined somewhat by demand for more comfort. The Caister camp became more popular with the lower middle-class, white collar workers seeking a different kind of seaside holiday away from the normal boarding house regime, but with the same comforts. The camp still attracted working-class campers as the cost of £2.5s for a week's stay in 1939 was still good value, and campers continued to provide their evening entertainment and community sing-alongs.27

Both the co-operative movement and trade unions were involved in the provision of holiday camps for their members, aiming to provide cheap worthwhile holidays by the sea. The general secretary of the Civil Service Clerical Association, W.J. Brown, was also inspired to set up a camp near Caister in 1924, after experiencing the restrictions of traditional seaside boarding houses. He had chalets built with electric light and running water with space for children, all of which were demanded by his white collar members.27 The camp was owned by the union, and sited in picturesque wooded grounds donated by Jeremiah Colman of the mustard family. The capital for constructing the camp had to raise commercially, as the offering of shares to union members proved unsuccessful. But the camp proved popular, and another was built at Hayling Island in 1930 to even higher standards ofcomfort.28

26   The Main Ofice and Shop at Caister Holiday Camp

 Among other trade unions involved in providing holidays for their members was the more militant National and Local Government Officers. It realized it would be popular to provide a range of services for its members that were cheaper than commercial providers, including mortgages, insurance, and holiday facilities. It opened a holiday camp at Croyde Bay in Devon in 1931 with various facilities including tennis courts, putting greens, a dining and entertainment hall and ninety-five huts or chalets. A further camp was opened in1933 at Cayton Bay near Scarborough which was even larger, with bowling greens, a children's playground and beach bungalows to encourage swimming and sunbathing.29

   These, and other examples of trade union involvement in holiday camps, were primarily concerned with providing cheap and comfortable holidays for their members, but there was also the underlying premise that healthy organized activity, preferably outdoors in the open air, was preferable to idly strolling along the promenade, sitting in a deck chair on the beach for spending time in amusement arcades. The campers rarely, if ever, left the camps during their one or two week stays, as everything was provided for them with set mealtimes, organized entertainment and plenty of competitions and events to keep the whole family occupied.

The Co-operative Society's holiday camps were started in 1911 with a camp at Rothesay in Scotland, where the guests slept in tents and the younger co-operative campers, at least, might have regarded sleeping in the open air as an invigorating and healthy way to spend their holidays. The Renfrewshire and United Cooperative Baking Society had a camp at Roseland and the bell-tents were pitched in the surrounding fields of a farm. It was so successful that the farm was purchased the next year for £600 and improvements were made. Permanent accommodation was soon in place, and after the war chalet accommodation for 400 campers was built.30

The Coventry Co-operative Society started with a camping party over the Whitsun holiday in 1929, and the following year opened a more permanent camp by the sea at Rhyl in North Wales. The accommodation was quite basic at first, consisting of converted railway carriages, ex-army huts and tents, but was still fully booked in July and August. This success encouraged the society to improve the site with sixty new chalets and more space. The enterprise was undertaken in a co-operative spirit, and run on a non-profit making lines, as it was subsidized by from the society's profits.31

The Worker's Travel Association was also established to provide communal holidays for the working-class in beautiful surroundings. Its founder was Cecil Rogerson wanted to encourage more international understanding and co-operation through foreign travel. The Great War had just ended, and there was a determination to ensure everything possible was done to preserve the hard-won peace. The WTA's executive included of trade unionist members, and it received patronage from leading members of the Labour Party such as Ernest Bevin and Margaret Bondfield. There were also links with the Holiday Fellowship and the Toynbee Hall settlement.32

From 1922 the WTA organized tours to Europe for workers at low costs, starting in France, but the standards did not always matched those advertised and there were complaints. The largely lower middle class clerks, trade union officials, and teachers did not expect to make their own beds or contribute to the cooking. The trade unions wanted better quality for their members, who were getting more materialistic in outlook. They saw no reason why being trade unionists, socialists, or Labour voters were not entitled to high standards of accommodation. The self-sufficient spartan holiday was no longer so appealing, and communal efforts and comradely greetings were increasingly limited to conferences and resolutions. And yet the holidays offered by the WTA were still expected to be low-priced and value for money, and in time the organization improved so that it became a major provider of foreign package holidays, even rivaling Thomas Cook.

Later it went into partnership with the Co-operative Wholesale Society to form Travco Camps Ltd, and built Rogerson Hall Holiday Centre in 1938 at Corton in Norfolk. This was a modern, well-designed and comfortable camp, while another at Westward Ho in Devon, was equally successful. Unlike the private enterprise holiday camps, the communal approach persisted, for example, with child-care shared by the campers or communally organized. The emphasis was still on equality rather than individuality, with no 'extra' services that could be paid for. The WTA also offered coach tours at home and abroad, stays at commercial hotels and guest houses, and activity holidays of all kinds.33

The flavor of early socialist idealism persisted among many working and middle-class holidaymakers up to the 1950s., but this gradually abated with improved living standards and growth in the holiday industry. The 'socialist holiday' providers found they were in a market diminishing in size, while commercial holiday camps like Butlins and Pontins had wider appeal. But the attractions for many of open-air holidays in scenic surroundings did not diminish and remained highly popular, even if the ideological basis for this did decline. As air travel came within the reach of families of even modest means, foreign package holidays to Spain and elsewhere became attainable and popular from the mid-1950s.

The socialist Left saw the natural landscape as a national amenity for all to enjoy, and this was carried over into Labour Party policy. While it was aware that the land was part of the national economy, a source of both food and employment, the party also tended to see it as a source of recreation for urban dwellers. It tried to reconcile these two potentially conflicting priorities with schemes that could possibly be justified under both headings, such as afforestation. The re-forestation of large tracts of unused landscape would provide employment and utilize a wasted resource, provide a useful product and also give opportunities for urban visitors to enjoy leisure activities in the new forests. The adoption of a policy for National Parks was also part of Labour's attempt to retain policies that designated land as a national resource for all the people to enjoy. As early as 1918 MacDonald was asserting the rights of the people to common land designated for social ownership. So plans to create National Parks echoed older socialist views of the countryside and its use. When he became Prime Minister in 1929 MacDonald set up a committee to consider the feasibility of creating one or more National Parks. The report was generally positive, and the party continued to promote the idea for national parks throughout the 1930s.34

The hope was for vast areas of land of great scenic beauty to be designated as great public parks for the enjoyment of all the people, on the model of the great Canadian and American parks. The assumption was that private ownership of land should not be a barrier to such a scheme, and also underlay the support of many socialists for the creation of the National Trust in a role as a manager of land for the public benefit. Some of the areas seen fit for designation as areas of outstanding national beauty were close to large population densities, such as the Peak District. For a long time ramblers, hill and mountain climbers had been drawn to the area for many years. Ideally a national park should not be too distant from the centres of population, but far enough for it to be seen as special and not as a 'glorified Hyde Park.'35

The uniqueness of the British landscape and the desire to be in was for many early socialists an important element of their leisure and holiday activities. The desire to go to places of great natural beauty determined the choice of location, and also the type of accommodation. The context of the trip or activity was important and chosen with care to be consistent with their beliefs and values. It was important to be in a natural environment and engage with these surroundings, with a minimum of commercial intervention. The hope was that they would derive spiritual refreshment, be able to put more material matters into perspective, and be re-energized to face the task of making a living and perhaps continue campaigning for a fairer and more equal society. These values also continued for a time to influence the more mass-market socialist workers holiday camps and tours. To this extent leisure and holiday activities were at one with living a life that signified commitment and belief in a cause. For a time 'leisure with a purpose' was a reality for thousands of people until rising materialism had its effect on class solidarity and socialist belief.

9   CONCLUSIONS

The early socialists in Britain saw the countryside and the natural world as inherently superior to the cities and towns that had resulted from industrialization and factory production. The countryside, large parts of which were still 'unspoilt', symbolized a freedom that the working-classes no longer enjoyed, 'enslaved' in factory production. Their urban lives consisted of long working hours, often in an unhealthy environment, with overcrowded and insanitary living conditions. The countryside represented both a contrast and a solution to the iniquities of urban capitalism. Its scenic beauty and fresh air compared favorably to the urban conditions that disfigured large swathes of Britain. It also represented a resource that could be utilized for leisure, and for more permanent settlement of one kind or another. These rural concerns were influenced by the romantic nostalgia for a Merrie England, partly mythical, but no less powerful as an inspiration motivation.

The land and access to it had always been at the heart of the early socialist project in Britain, with the imperative of redressing the injustices of monopoly land ownership, and lack of access for the mass of the people. This festering sense of injustice was mixed with a strong sense of loss, and nostalgia for the rural past of a happy and contented people living their lives freely. Whether justified or not, this vision strongly influenced socialist writers, notably William Morris and Robert Blatchford, who were full of righteous indignation about it. For them repossession of the land was a core element in the recreation of 'Merrie England,' and a necessary precondition for a democratic socialist society to flourish. It became a powerful influence on socialists for over sixty years, and underlay much of their thinking and action. The theme fed into Labour Party policies to manage and conserve the land, ensure it became a resource for planned settlement and leisure, so that everyone would be able to live harmoniously in 'England's green and pleasant land.'

These utopian ideals were criticized at the time for a lack of realism and tendency to divert attention away from concrete solutions to the problems of urban life such as massive slum clearance, improved urban amenities and safer work environments. As such these utopian socialist could be accused of looking backwards as inspiration for creating a nostalgic utopia out of touch with the dynamics of modern capitalism and unable to cope with it. Even 'municipal socialism' was criticized by Lenin as a reactionary utopia and bringing about socialism piecemeal that was hopeless. and Chamberlain in Birmingham was looking away from the fundamental ills of the economic system.1 Much the same could be said for those who took their own initiatives to create self-sufficient communities, leasing or purchasing land communally with the aim of creating their own small utopias, free from dependency and exploitation.

In hindsight socialist utopian schemes of one kind or another can be seen as naïve, but to the participants they were an adventure in an alternative form of living that at least held out the promise of a better life. They were not revolutionaries, and neither did they seek anything so ambitious as replacing capitalism with their own brand of social organization, but were putting into practice, with a few other like-minded people, a way of life that combined principle with contentment. As we have seen, these experimental communities met with varying degrees of success, some succeeded and others were unable to survive financially, or found the realities of human nature counter-productive. In any case, they were in a long tradition of radical assertion of the right to live freely as they wished, in small communities, fraternal and communitarian. Inspired less by ideology than a strong belief in the human capacity for cooperation, if uncorrupted by the selfishness and greed engendered by capitalist materialism or party political intrigue.

There were others who tried to combine their socialist beliefs with leisure activity, including cyclists, campers, hikers and sports of all kind. They formed mutual support groups, some more overtly political than others, but all sharing the belief that humanity and nature were inextricably linked. Being in the open air, amid scenic beauty had a transformative effect on the human spirit, and put people more in touch with their common humanity. Many open-air socialists had little time for party politics, but sought to live naturally and fraternally with their colleagues, friends and neighbours in so far as this was possible in a capitalist society. They hoped for the time when a fully socialist society would arrive, but in the meantime lived their lives as consistent with their beliefs as possible, including leisure and social activities.

There was also an interest in making connections with the rural traditions and customs of the past including music, dance, folk traditions and crafts. These rural activities could also be practiced in the town, and help people re-connect with their rural past and even inspire explorations into the countryside. They were seen as authentic symbols of socialist ruralism, discovering and reviving them an important way of re-kindling working-class culture, reconnecting the urban masses with their own rural past. The folk traditions, songs and customs reflected the changing seasons, and the rhythms of agricultural life, celebrating the fruits as well as the hardships of life on the land and the struggle to make a living from it. When the Labour Party was formed some socialists were aghast at the decision to pursue the parliamentary route to a socialist society. None more so than Robert Blatchford who made it plain in the *Clarion* that this was not the way to build a New Jerusalem, with the inevitable personal ambition, party manoeuvring and compromise of principle. He believed attempting to impose socialism from the top down would never work, the only hope was for the people to build a new world for themselves from the grass- roots up. For a time many committed themselves to doing so, and early socialism had many of the features of a new religion, with the all the spiritually transformative effects of a new faith. To-day, with the word 'socialism' itself virtually expunged from the lexicon of the modern Labour Party, the profound belief in its inherent virtues by many people might seem remote, but for a time it was the vital element in their lives.

The antagonism of early socialists to urban life and the effects of industrialization helps explain their emotional connection to open air life and the countryside. It was about repossessing the land, rivers and lakes which had once been pristine during a pre-industrial 'golden age', but many of which were then despoiled with mining, quarrying, and manufacturing waste. In addition, the health of the workers had been damaged, and their sensibilities blunted by squalid living and working conditions. By re-claiming ownership and access,

an ancient wrong would be redressed, but would prepare the way for
everyone to enjoy all the facilities and blessings of nature. But this
time not as tenants but as free men and women with the leisure to
fully appreciate and enjoy the glories of the landscape.

The idealization of the countryside in the writing of the left was
reinforced by images of pastoral scenes in which thatched cottages,
villages, ancient yokels and cheerful farm workers predominated. The
idealized images of gardens were heavy with symbolism in the
illustrations of Walter Crane, and continued during the inter-war
years in photographs and illustrations that continued this vision.
Typical were the photographs of the countryside in the left-wing
Daily Herald that showed picturesque villages, peacefully grazing
livestock, and tranquil meadows. In the 'Countryman's Log' column,
the rural subjects were always benign and comforting such as bread-
making and bee-keeping rather than the real problems of running a
farm and making it pay.2

A belief in the countryside as a source of spiritual refreshment lay
at the basis of the 'open air' movement, and in the growth of open air
activities of all kinds between the wars. Until a permanent socialist
society arrived, excursions or temporary stays in the countryside were
a way of finding at least some physical or moral uplift. Being in the
open air invested all kinds of activities for socialists with a legitimacy
they might otherwise have lacked, whether it was rambling, camping,
playing cricket or going on holiday, or country dancing. Those with
sufficient commitment and means joined rural based communities to
colonize the land, and attempted to live a communal life based on
socialist principles. This chimed with Labour Party policy before
1914 which supported wider land-ownership, free and independent
rural artisans. There was also the widespread belief that farming
efficiency could be best promoted by a 'back to the land' movement
of smallholdings and allotments.3

The land colonies that were formed before and after the Great War
had mixed success, but they were all radical in their determination to
throw off the constraints of capitalism and forge a new kind of
economic life. While seeking to break with the present, they also
looked back with nostalgia to a way of life with roots in the distant
past. Going back to the land, using basic or almost primitive methods
of cultivation in some cases, making their own furniture, growing

their own food and sharing surpluses was their way of creating this new society, however small and modest.

After the 1918 the attitude to the land by the socialist left was influenced by the relative economic decline of farming. There were depressed prices, cheap food imports, agricultural unemployment and a consequent effect on rural life. At the same time the national economy seemed to be undergoing a second bout of industrialization based on electricity and mass production, which seemed to encroach increasingly on the un-spoilt countryside. Whatever the improvement in living standards of the urban working class from this new industrialism, many socialists were alarmed at the overspill of factory growth, major road building, and suburban housing sprawl. There was also an increase in the monopoly ownership of land, with the vast estates by private landlords and commercial companies, adding to the concentration of land ownership, even while the influence of the traditional landed gentry was declining. The focus of the left went from attacking the landed aristocracy to concentrating on the development and control of land use, finding ways of protecting farm land and landscape from despoliation, and to protect access and use by the mass of the population.4

The desire to be both in the countryside and part of it, derived from the anti-urban sentiments of many on the socialist Left, a loathing of slum-housing, overcrowding, industrial pollution, all seen as the result of unfettered capitalism. The countryside was, in contrast, pristine and represented as a source of release and an escape. The revival in the popularity of the 'open air' movement between the wars in the form of rambling, cycling, camping, as well as land settlement, was a continuation of this belief inherited from early socialism. The idealization of the countryside, made them particularly sensitive to the consequences of unregulated rural economic development, increasing in motorized transport, new construction, pollution and noise. At the same time the countryside was seen as a resource for food production, new towns re-settlement and afforestation. This potential conflict was resolved, not entirely satisfactorily, by advocating more planning, regulation and education to try to preserve the best qualities of the countryside and limit access on strictly conditional terms.

Rambling, camping, and garden cities were approved forms of rural colonization, because they could be planned and controlled, and had a self-improving function. Other traditional country pursuits were disparaged, such as the game 'sports' of hunting, fishing and shooting. These were popular among the landed classes, including a few left-wing sympathizers and supporters. Charles Trevelyan enjoyed shooting on his estate, and Cyril Joad was an enthusiastic fox hunter when he could borrow a horse from his host at a country house weekend. His one-time patron Henry Harben, a Labour supporter and fellow Fabian, argued that game-breeding for hunting helped to preserve traditional wildlife, while shooting and fox-hunting were part of the local rural economy which provided employment for the estate workers and local villagers, paid good wages and the chance of a good lunch.5

The politicization of rural access meant that the social purpose of leisure became a socialist priority. The hikers, ramblers, cyclists, and others we have discussed, asserted their right to enjoy the countryside and to do so on their own terms. It had to be defended against commercial interests, and areas of outstanding national beauty protected. The view that the landscape belonged to the people for their pleasure and edification remained a constant, and a vision of 'Merrie England' lived on 'in which every Englishmen will live within reasonable distance of green fields instead of in the heart of the slums.'5 There were strong elements of class-war rhetoric involved in these prescriptions for more regulation, planning and control. The need to educate the people was clearly a priority, and despite the sometimes patronizing tone used, it was a well-intentioned aim to ensure people used the natural environment as an invaluable but finite resource.

Some of these objectives were shared by non-socialist organizations between the wars, as threats to the countryside became increasingly clear. It helped to see the creation of the Council for the Preservation of Rural England, the National Trust and the Ramblers Association, organizations that shared many of the preservationist impulses of the Left. Apart from defending and conserving the best of rural heritage against the ravages of the modern trade and commerce, the hope was that the built heritage of country houses, gardens and parkland would be made available to the people. The aim of mass participation took other forms, from camping and gardening, to rambling and holidays and included setting up national parks as well as accessing great country houses with their parks and gardens. The instinct, however, was always the same: asserting the democratic right of the people for access.

In 1936 the Council for the Preservation of Rural England made a short film in which it made the case for the creation of National Parks, something socialists had supported for years. The film is remarkable, coming from a non-political organization, for the socialist messages it contained, notably the right of free access to sites of natural beauty for all the people in town or country whatever their background or occupation. This birthright was seen as seriously threatened by the enormous social and economic changes taking place, and only designated parks, protected and supervised by statute, would ensure their continued protection.[6]

By the mid-1930s, the health and fitness movement had been added to the open-air movement, as the government realized the need for a physically fit population. The trade unions and the co-operative movement had also expanded their orbit to include holidays for their members. The employed working-class and lower middle-classes, were seeing a rise in real wages and paid holidays, and expected higher standards of comfort. The old socialist preference of opting for plain living, now had far less appeal, as did many of the attitudes of the early socialist towards the outdoor life. Although many of the open-air activities that had so engaged the early socialists continued in popularity after 1945, it was in a less overtly political manner. The struggle for access to the countryside continued, but many of the battles had been won such as the official protection of areas of outstanding national beauty. The work of the Ministry of Works and National Trust in preserving buildings, parks and monuments was expanding.

In 1945 the war had ended with the election a Labour government with a large overall majority for the first time, and with mass popular support for the creation of a welfare state. The country and its people were exhausted and the national finances almost bankrupted, and it was clear that the way to create a more equal and fairer society was through a powerful Labour Party willing to implement a socialist programme. By 1950, reforms were in place that few socialists had thought possible in the pre-war years of drift and torpor. But in this new focus on 'welfarism', nationalization, and economic planning, some of the old idealism about the countryside and the open air, and the role they should play in everyone's life, receded as deference to the state increased and individuals and groups seemed less ready to create their own arcadias.

Notes

1. Fraternity in the Open Air

1   William Morris, *News from Nowhere* (1890)
2   Keith Taylor & John K. Walton, *Constructing Cultural Tourism: John Ruskin and the Tourist Gaze* p. 155
3   Gillian Darley, *Octavia Hill: Social Reformer and Founder of the National Trust* (2004) p. 34
4   Robert Blatchford, *Merrie England* (1893) pp. 17-18
5   Tony Judge, *Tory Socialist: Robert Blatchford and Merrie England* (2013) p. 62
6   *County Standard* (1963) p. 85
7   Ann Laurence 'The Ranter Poems' *The Review o English Studies* 31, 121 p.56-59
8   Chris Waters, *British Socialists and the Politics of Popular Culture* (1990) p. 171
9   Ramsay MacDonald, *Wonderings and Excursions* (1925) p.63
10 Clare V.J. Griffiths, *Labour and the Countryside* (2007) pp. 27-28
11 *Merrie England* pp. 8-9
12 see Stephen Yeo, 'A New Life; the Religion of Socialism in Britain, 1883-1896' *History Workshop Journal* no.3 1977
13 Morna O'Neill, 'Walter Crane's Floral Fantasy-The Garden in Arts and Craft Politics' *Garden History* vol.135 no. 2 Winter 2008 pp. 296-297
14 *The Clarion* 16 February 1895
15 'Walter Crane's Floral Fantasy' p. 298
16 *Ibid*
17 C.E.M. Joad, *The Pleasure of Being Oneself* (1951) p. 47
18 Alun Hawkins, 'The Decline of the Countryside: in *The British Countryside Between the Wars* p. 14
19 *Labour and the Countryside* p. 293
20 *Ibid* p. 297
21 Ina Zweininger-Bargieloska, *Managing the Body: Beauty Health and Fitness in Britain* 1880-1939 (2010) p. 330

2 Clarion Clubs

1   *The Clarion* 12 December 1891
2   Robert Blatchford, *Merrie England* (1893) p.18-19
3   Stephen Koss, *The Political Press in Britain* (1984) p.93
4   *The Clarion* October 1894
5   *Ibid*
6   *The Scout,* March 1895
7   *The Clarion,* 6 October 1894
8   *The Clarion,* 1 June 1895
9   Dennis Pye, *Fellowship is Life: The Story of the Clarion Cycling Clubs* (2004) pp.18-1

10   *Ibid* pp.21-26

11   *The Clarion,* June 1897

12   *Ibid*

13   *Fellowship is Life* pp.79-81

14   *Ibid*

15   *Ibid*

16   *The Clarion* March 1931

17   *Ibid*

18   C. Stella Davies, *North Country Bred; A Working Class Family Chronicle* (1963) p.85

19   *Fellowship is Life*

20   *The Clarion* 24 August 1917

21   H. Briercliffe, 'Cycling is Political' *Clarion Cyclist* August 1936

22   *The Clarion,* October 1937

23   *Clarion Cyclist,* January 1937

24   C.E.M. Joad, *A Charter for Ramblers* (1934) p-.36-37; *Clarion Cyclist* Sept. 1937

25   Quoted in Juliet Gardner, *The Thirties, an intimate decade* (2010) p.249

26   Quoted in Denis Pye, *Fellowship is Life: The NEW Clarion Cycle Club 1895-1995* (1995) p.50

3. Folk Arts, Gardens, Education & Schools

1   Robert Blatchford, *Merrie England* (1893) p.7

2   *Ibid* p.5

3   Roy Judge, 'May Day and Merrie England' *Folklore* 102/2 (1991) p.141

4   *New Leader* May 1923

5   *Labour Organizer* January 1938

6   Dave Harper, 'May Cecil Sharp be praised?' *History Workshop Journal* 14 Aug. 1982 p.60

7   Maud Karpeles, *Cecil Sharp: His Life and Work* (1967) pp.67-68

8   Alec Hunter, 'Back to Merrie England' *Labour Magazine* August 1923

9   see Dave Harper 'May Cecil Sharp be praised' *History Workshop* 14 August 1982

10   see Alan Frogley, 'Ralph Vaughan Williams (1872-1958) Oxford Dictionary of National Biography; J. Onderdonk, 'Ralph Vaughan Williams, Folk Song Collecting, English Nationalism and the rise of professional society (Ph.D diss. New York University 1998)

11   *The Spectator* , November 1919

12   Alan Crawford, C.R. Ashbee: Architect, Designer and Romantic Socialist (1981) p. 211-213

13   *Ibid* p. 84-85

14   *Ibid* p. 101

15   *Ibid*

16   Reginald Groves, *Conrad Noel and the Thaxted Movement* (1967) p.68

17   Clive Aslet, *Villages of Britain: The 500 villages that made the countryside* (2010)

18   Leslie Paul, *The Folk Trail* p.22

19   Clare V.J. Griffiths, *Labour and the Country* (2007) p.98
20   see Brian Morris, 'Ernest Thompson and the Origins of the Woodcraft
      movement' *Journal of Contemporary History* 5.2 (1970) pp.183-194; David
      Prynne, 'The Woodcraft Folk and the Labour Movement 1925-1970' *Journal
      of Contemporary History* 18 (1983) pp.79-95
21   Mary Davis, *Fashioning a New World: a History of the Woodcraft Folk* (2000) p.25
22   Leslie Paul, *The Early Days of the Woodcraft Folk* (1980) p.9
23   *Ibid* p.63
24   *Fashioning a New World* p.59
25   C. Steedman, *Children, Culture and Class in Britain: Margaret MacMillan* 1860-1931
      (1990) p.28ff
26   Margaret McMillan, *The Camp Schools* (1917) p.79
27   Margaret McMillan, *What is the New Open Air Nursery? (1910) p.3*
28   Margaret McMillan, *Nursery Education* (1919) p.3
29   *Ibid* pp.23-24
30   *Ibid* p.25
31   *Ibid* pp. 26-27
32   *Ibid* p.30
33   *Ibid*
34   R. Cooper ed., *In the Name of the Child: Health & Welare 1880-1940* (1992)
35   quoted in Deborah Gorman, 'Bertrand and Dora Russell and Beacon Hill
      School' *Journal of Bertrand Russell Studies* 25 summer 2004 p.40
36   Kevin Manton, *Socialism and Education in Britain* 1883-1902 p57
37   *Ibid*
38   *The Clarion,* 15 July, 7 Oct, 18 Nov. 1899
39   *Socialism and Education in Britain* p.112
40   *Ibid* p.117
41   *Ibid* p.122
42   Beacon Hill School Prospectus 1926
43   Michael Young, *The Elmhirsts of Dartington: The Creation of a Utopian Community*
      (1982) p.82
44   *Ibid*

4 Co-operative Communities and Land Settlements

1   Dennis Hardy, *Utopian England, Community Experiments* 1900-1945 (2007) p.204
2   quoted in C. Tsuzuki, *Edward Carpenter 1844-1929, Prophet of Human Fellowship*
      (1980) p.50
3   *Utopian England* p.69
4   *Ibid* p.23
5   *Ibid* p.25
6   *The New Order* January 1927
7   Charlotte Alston, 'Tolstoy's Guiding Light' *History Today* Oct 2010
8   *Seed Time* 30 January 1894
9   W.H.G. Armytage, 'J.C.Kenworthy and the Tolstoyan Community in England'

American Journal of Economic & Social History no 4 July 1957 p.394

10 *The Clarion* 20 August 1898

11 'J.C. Kenworthy and the Tolstoyan Community in England' p.396

12 *The New Order* February 1899

13 see Nellie Shaw, *Whiteways: A Colony in the Cotswolds* (1935)

14 *Morning Star* 12 March 1999

15 *Utopian England* pp.174-175

16 *Ibid* p.24

17 Thomas Linehan, *Modernism and British Socialism* (2014) p.129

18 *Ibid* p.132

19 Margaret Willes, *The Gardens of the British Working Class* 2014 p.137

20 David Middleton Murry quoted in W.H.G. Armytage, *Heavens Below: Cooperative Experiment sin England* 1560-1960 (1961) p.397

21 John Middleton Murry, 'Community and Totalitarianism' *The Adelphi* Nov. 1941

22 George Woodcock, *The Basis of Communal Living* (1947) p.227

23 Colin Middleton Murry, *Shadows in the Grass* (1977) p. 227

24 *Ibid* p.42

25 cited in Theo Barker, *The Long March of Everyman* 1950-1960 (1978)

23 Colin Middleton Murry, *Shadows in the Grass* (1977) p,227

24 *Ibid* p.42

25 cited in Theo Barker, *The Long March of Everyman* 1950-1960 (1978)

26 Colin Ward & Dennis Hardy, *Arcadia for All* (1984) p.9

27 *Ibid* p.9-11

28 C.E.M. Joad, *The Book of Joad* p.137-138; see also *The Untutored Townsman's Invasion of the Country* (1946)

29 *Arcadia for All* p.27-30

5 Garden Cities and Allotments

1 Stanley Buder, *Visionaries and Planners* (1990) p.81

2 Ebenezer Howard, *Tomorrow: A Peaceful Pathway to Real Reform*

3 J.W. Mackail, *The Life of William Morris* p.302

4 *Daily Herald* 24 July 1933

5 *Visionaries and Planners* p.118

6 R. Fishman, *Urban Utopias* n the twentieth Century (1977) p.81

7 E. Bonham Carter, 'Planni ng and Development of Garden Cities' *Town Planning Review* vol. 121 no 4 pp. 362-376

8 Mervyn Miller, *English Garden Cities: An Introduction* (2010) p1

9 'Democratic Dilemmas, Plannig and Ebenezer Howard's Garden City' *Planning Perspectives* vol. 19 pp409-433

10 see Jonathan Glancey, 2Silver End Housing Estate" in *20th Century Architecture: The Structures that Shaped the Century* (1998)

11 Mervyn Miller, *Hampstead Garden Suburb* (2006)

12 Margaret Willes, *The Gardens of the Working Class* (2014) p.266

13 Lesley Acton, 'Allotment Gardens: Reflection on the History, Community and

Self' *Proceedings of the Institute of Archeology* 21 December 2011 pp46-58

14 *The Gardens of the Working Class,* p. 276

15 Clare V.J. Griffiths, *Labour and the Countryside* (2007) p296

16 Elizabeth Scott, 'Cockney Plots' in D. Brien et al (ed) *Gardening for Everyone: Cultivating Wisdom* (2010) p.114

17 *Ibid*

18 'Allotment Gardens for the Unemployed' (www.allotmentresources.org) p.1

19 *Ibid* P.2

20 'Cockney Plots' p. 115

21 *The Gardens of the Working Class* p.115

22 Cockney Plots

23 *The Garden of the Working Class*

6 Summer Schools and Country Houses

1 see Edward R. Pease, *The History of the Fabian Society* (1925) pp199-202

2 cited in Burrow, *University Adult Education* p.68

3 *Fabian News* Sept 1911

4 *Fabian News* Oct. 1911

5 *Ibid* March 1907

6 Fabian Summer School Prospectus 1915

7 *Fabian News* vol.35 no.110 October 1925

8 *The History of the Fabian Society* p.200

9 Tony Judge, *Radio Philosopher, The Radical Life of Cyril Joad* (2012) p.39

10 C.E.M. Joad, *A Year More or Less* (1948) pp.197-200

11 *Ibid*

12 Report, ILP Annual Conference, April 1925 pp24-25

13 *Labour League of Youth Magazine* February 1924

14 Betty Boothroyd, *Boothroyd, the Autobiography* (2002) pp.76-77

15 *Radio Philosopher* p.41

16 *Ibid*

17 N. MacKenzie, *The Letters of Beatrice and Sydney Webb* vol.3 1912-1947 pp.171-2

18 www.britishpathe.com Labour Party Meeting 1923

19 Keith Laybourn, *Fifty key Figures in 20th Century British Politics* (2002) p.187

20 Sushula Anand, *Daisy: The Life and Loves of the Countess Warwick* (2009) p.268

21 Margaret Cole, *The Story of Fabian Socialism* (1961) pp222-227

22 Adrian Tinniswood, *The Long Weekend* (2016)

23 Clare V.J. Griffiths, *Labour in the Countryside* (2007) p.297

24 A.J.A. Morris, *C.P. Trevelyan 1870-1968: Portrait of a Radical* (1977) p173

25 *Ibid* p.162

26 Christopher Goulding, 'The People's Friend in the Country' *The Northumbrian* Spring 1992

27 *Ibid*

28 D. Jeremiah, 'Dartington Hall: a landscape for an experiment in rural

reconstruction' in *The British Countryside between the Wars: Decline or Revival* (2006)

29 *Ibid*

7 Rambling and Camping

1 Stephen G. Jones, *Sport, Britain and the Working Class* (1988) p. 168
2 C.E.M. Joad, *A Charter for Ramblers* (1934) p. 12
3 Howard Hill, *Freedom to Roam: The Struggle for Access to Britain's Moors and Mountains* (1980) p. 32
4 Tom Stephenson, *Forbidden Land: the Struggle for Access to Mountain and Moorland* (1989 p. 89
5 Paul Salveson, *Will ye Come O Sunday Morning? The 1896 Battle for Winter Hill* (1982)
6 Ramsay MacDonald, *Wanderings and Excursions* 1925 pp. 75-76
7 *Ibid* p. 39
8 Ramsay MacDonald, *At Home and Abroad* (1936) p. 92
9 MacDonald, *The Socialist Message* (1911) p. 248
10 Joad, *Untutored Townsman's Invasion of the Countryside* (1946) p. 48
11 *A Charter for Ramblers* p. 30
12 Joad, *The Book of Joad* (1939) pp. 200-204
13 *Ibid* p.89
14 *Ibid*
15 *Ibid* p. 96
16 Oliver Coburn, *Youth Hostel Story* (1950) p. 29
17 Tim Neal & Simon Neal, *Youth Hostels of England and Wales* 1931-1998 (1993) p.23
18 YHA Handbook 1939
19 *The Spirit of the YHA* p.47
20 *Youth Hostel Story* p. 187
21 C.E.M. Joad, *More Opinions* (1946) p. 18
22 Clare V.J. Griffiths, *Labour and the Country* (2007) p. 90
23 Tony Judge, *Radio Philosopher, The Radical Life of Cyril Joad* (2012) p. 107
24 *The Book of Joad* p. 156
25 *Ibid*
26 *A Charter for Ramblers* pp. 157-158
27 *A Charter for Ramblers* pp. 144
28 Hazel Constance 'Thomas Hiron Holding' *Oxford Dictionary of National Biography*
29 G.A. Cohen, *Why Not Socialism* (2009) pp.1-10
30 *Ibid*
31 J. Field, Alternative Living Alternative Learning: The Grith Fyrd Movement in England in the 1930s' in *The Rise and Fall of Adult Education Instututions and Social Movements* (2000)
32 www.britishpathe.com/video/army-of-peace

33   J. Field, *Working Men's Bodies: Work Camps in Britain,* 1880-1914 (2013)
34   *Ibid*

8   Sport, Fitness and Holiday Leisure

1   S. Pierson, *British Society: The Journey from Factory to Politics* (1979) p. 168
2   Jones, *Workers at Play: A Social and Economic History of Leisure* 1918-1939 (1986)
      p. 75
3   *New Dawn* 8 December 1923
4   *Daily Herald* 13 April 1923
5   *Workers at Play* p. 75
6   *Ibid* p. 76
7   Thomas Linehan, *Communism in Britain: From the Cradle to the Grave* (2007) p. 117
8   *Daily Worker* 27 January 1932
9   *Workers at Play* p. 107
10 David Berry, 'Workers' Wimbledon' *Prospect* July 2017 pp60-63
11 *The Independent* 7 July 2013
12 Jon Henderson, *The Life of Fred Perry* (2011) p.125
13 *Co-operative News* 21 July 1932
14 *Workers at Play* p. 112
15 *The Clarion* 23 April 1892
16 *Ibid* 6 August 1892
17 Robert Snape, 'The National Reading Union, 1889-1930' *Journal of Victorian Culture* 2002 7 (1) pp. 86-11
18 Harvey Taylor, *A Claim on the Countryside: A History of the British Outdoor*
19 *Ibid*
20 *Ibid* p. 207
21 Susan Barton, *Working Class Organizations and Popular Culture* 1840-1970 p. 144
22 *Comradeship* 21 December 1908
23 *Ibid* February 1909
24 Keith Hanley & John K. Walton, *Constructing Cultural Tourism: John Ruskin and the Tourist Gaze* (2010) p. 170
25 *Working Class Organizations and Popular Culture* p. 146
26 Colin Ward & Dennis Hardy, *Goodnight Campers* (1986) p. 16
27 *Working Class Organizations and Popular Culture* p. 147
28 *Ibid* pp. 151-151
29 *Ibid*
30 *Goodnight Campers* p. 43
31 *Ibid* pp. 46-47
32 *Working Class Organizations* p. 154
33 *Ibid* p. 158
34 Clare V.J. Griffiths, *Labour and the Country* (2007) p. 315
35 *Ibid*

9 Conclusions

1 V.I. Lenin, *Municipalisation of the Land*(1907)
2 *Daily Herald* 24 and 26 July, 15 August 1933
3 M. Tichekar, 'Socialists, Labour and the Land': the response of the Labour
    Party to the Land Campaign of Lloyd George before the First World War'
    Twentieth Century British History 8 (1997) pp. 127-144
4 M. Tichekar, 'The Labour Party and Land Reform in the Inter-War period' *Rural
    History* 13 (2002) pp. 85-98
5 Henry D. Harben, *The Rural Problem* (1913) pp. 97-98
6 'Rural England' Council for the Preservation of Rural England Film 1938
    www.youtube.com

Bibliography

Primary Sources

Clarion Papers, (Labour History Archive Manchester)
Fabian Archive, (LSE)
George Lansbury Papers (BLPES)
LCC Parks Department Records (National Archives)
Ramsay MacDonald Papers (National Archives)
YHA Historical Archive (University of Birmingham)
National Cycle Archive (University of Warwick)
BL National Newspaper Archive

Secondary Sources

Matthew de Abaitua, *The Art of Camping* (2011)
Robert Beaver, *The Garden City Utopia* (1988)
John Belchem, *Industrialization and the Working Class: The English Experience* (1991)
Robert Blatchford, *Merrie England* (1893); *The Sorcery Shop* (1917)
Paul Brassley et al (ed.) *The English Countryside Between the Wars: Decline or Revival?* (2006)
Marc Brodie, *The Politics of the Poor: The East End of London* 1885-1914 (1992)
Alistair Bonnet, *Left in the Past, Radicalism and the Politics of Nostalgia* (2010)
Jeremy Burchardt, *The Allotment Movement in England* 1793-1873 (2002); *Paradise Lost: Rural Idylls and Social Change since 1800* (2002)
Arthur Burns, 'Beyond the Red Vicar: Community and Christian Socialism in Thaxted Essex 1910-1984 *History Workshop Journal* Spring 2013 75 (1) pp101-124
Susan Burton, *Working Class Organizations and Tourism* 1840-1970 (2005)
Anne Marie Chatelet 'A Breath of Fresh Air: Open Air Schools in Europe' in Maura Gutman: *Designing Modern Childhoods: History Space and Material Culture of Children* (2008)
H. Gustav Claus & Valentine Cunningham, *Ecology and the Left: The Red and the Green* (2012)
G.A. Cohen, *Why Not Socialism?* (2009)
A. Crawford, *C.R. Ashbee: Architect, Designer, Romantic Socialist* (1982)
W.B. Curry, *The School* (1934)
Gillian Darley, *Octavia Hill: Social Reformer and the Founder of the National Trust* (2004)
Mary Davis, *Fashioning a New World: A History of the Woodcraft Folk* (2000)
Alan Delgado, *The Annual Outing and Other Excursions* (1976)
John Field, *Workingmen's Bodies: Work Camps in Britain* 1880-1914 (2013)
Geoffrey Glasby, *Mass Trespass on Kinder Scout in 1932* (2014)
J.M. Golby & A.W. Purdue, *The Civilization of the Crowd: Popular Culture in England*

1750-1900 (1984) rev. ed. (1999)

Clare V. Grifiths, *Labour and the Country* (2007)

Trevor Griffiths, *The Lancashire Working Class* 1880-1930 (2001)

Reginald Grove, *Conrad Noel and the Thaxted Movement* (1967)

Keith Hanley & John K. Walton, *Constructing Cultural Tourism: John Ruskin and the Tourist Gaze* (2010)

Dennis Hardy, *Utopian England: Community Experiments* 1900-1945 (2000)

Brian Harrison, 'Traditions of Respectability in the British Labour Party' in *Peaceable Kingdom*(1982)

Jon Henderson, *The Last Champion: The Life of Fred Perry* (2011)

James Hinton, *Labour and Socialism: A History of the British Labour Movement* 1867-1974(1983)

Janice Holland, British Home Arts and Industries 1880-1914

Richard Holt, *Sport and the British: A Modern History* (1989)

David Howell, *British Workers and the Independent Labour Party* 1888-1939 (1983)

Martin Hoyles, *The Story of Gardening* (1991)

Stephen G. Jones, *Workers at Play : A Social and Economic History of Leisure* 1918-1939 (1986); *Sport Britain and the Working Class* (1988)

Tony Judge, *Radio Philosopher:The Radical Life of Cyril Joad* (2012); *Tory Socialist: Robert Blatchford and Merrie England* (2013)

Thomas P. Linehan, *Communism in Britain: From the Cradle to the Grave* (2007); *Modernism and British Socialism*(2014)

Fiona MacCarthy, *Simple Life: C.R.. Ashbee in the Cotswolds* (1981)

Leah Manning, *A Life in Education* (1972)

Kevin Manton, *Socialism and Education in Britain* 1883-1902 (2001); 'Fellowship and Ruskin Home School, a turn of the century social and educational experiment' *Journal of History of Education* vol. 26. 47

John Marriott, *The Culture of Labourism: The East End Between the Wars* (1991)

David Matless, *Landscape and Englishness* (1998)

A.M. Mc Briar, *Fabian Socialism and English Politics* 1884-1918 (1962)

R.I. McKibbin, *Ideologies of Class: Social Relations in Britain* 1888-1970 (1978)

Mervyn Miller, *Letchworth* (2005); *Hampstead Garden Suburb* (2006)

Roger Moore, *The Emergence of the Labour Party* 1880-1924 (1978)

A.J.A. Morris, *C.P. Trevelyan 1870-1958: Portrait of a Radical*(1977)

John Middleton Murry, *Community Farm* (1953)

Morna O'Neill, *Walter Crane: The Arts and Crafts, People and Politics 1875-1890*(2010)

Jason Orton & Ken Worpole, *The New English Landscape* (2013)

Edward R. Pease, *The History of the Fabian Society* (1925)

Harold Perkin, *The Structured Crowd* (1981)

Martin Pugh, *Speak for England: A New History of the Labour Party* (2011)

Jack Putterill, *Conrad Noel, Prophet and Priest* (1962)

Dennis Pye, *Fellowship is Life: The Story of the Clarion Cycling Club* (2004)

Shiela Rowbotham, *Edward Carpenter, A Life of Liberty and Love* (2008)

Raphael Samuel, *Village Life and Labour* (1975); *The Lost World of British Communism* (2006)

Marion Shoard, *This Land is Our Land: The Struggle for the British Countryside* (1997)

Joseph R. Starr, 'The summer schools and other educational activities of the British socialist Group' *American Political Science Review* 30 1936 pp. 956-974

C. Steedman, *Children, Culture & Class in Britain: Margaret McMillan 1860-1931* (1990)

Tom Stephenson, *Forbidden Land: The Struggle for Access to Mountain and Moorland* (1989)

Harvey Taylor, *A Claim on the Countryside: A History of the Outdoor Movement* (1997

Joy Thacker, *Whiteway: The Social History of a Tolstoyan Community* (1993)

Adrian Tinniswood, *The Long Weekend, Life in the English Country House 1918-39* (2016)

Selina Todd, *The People: The Rise and Fall of the British Working Class* 1910-2010 (2014)

Chris Waters, *British Socialism and the Politics of Popular Culture 1884-1914* (1990)

John Walton, *The British Seaside Holiday and Resorts in the Twentieth Century* (2000)

Colin Ward & Dennis Hardy, *Arcadia for All* (1984); *Goodnight Campers* (1987)

Chris Water, *British Socialism and the Politics of Popular Culture* (1990)

Michelle Webb, *The Labour League of Youth, An Account of the Labour Party's Failure to Sustain a Successful Youth Organization* (2011)

Martin J. Weiner, *English Culture and the Decline of the Industrial Spirit* (1981)

Margaret Willes, *The Gardens of the British Working Class* (2014)

Francis Williams, *Journey Into Adventure: The History of the Worker's Holiday Association* (1960)

F. Wilmot & P. Saul, *A Breath of Fresh Air: Birmingham's Open Air Schools 1911-1970*

Matthew Worley (ed.), *Labour's Grass Roots: Essays on the Activities of Local Labour Parties and Members,* 1918-1945 (2008)

Eileen and Stephen Yeo, 'A New Life: The Religion of Socialism in Britain, 1883-1896' *History Workshop Journal* No. 4 1977

Michael Young, *The Elmhirsts of Dartington: The Creation of a Utopian Community* (1982)

Illustrations

Acknowledgements

I would like to thank staff of the following for their help and guidance: the British Library, National Newspaper Reference Library then at Colindale, the London of Economics and Political Science Library, and the libraries of the universities of Birmingham and Warwick, Nuffield College Oxford and the Labour History Archive in Manchester.

Index

Tony Judge has held posts in UK and US universities for many years as a professor and Dean. He was a postgraduate student at LSE, and has been a Teacher Fellow at SOAS, University of London.